© Copyright 2020 by Michael Malone.
All rights reserved. No part of this book may be reproduced in any form or by any electronic or mechanical means, including information storage and retrieval systems, without permission in writing from the author Michael Malone except by a reviewer who may quote brief passages in a review.

DEAD SERIOUS

WRITTEN BY MICHAEL MALONE

Thank Ya! :)

FOREWORD
By **Brad Garrett**

The first time I saw Michael Malone perform was at my comedy club in Las Vegas. I remember thinking to myself, 'How the fuck does this guy make a living!?' (You can say stuff like that about a fellow comedian when you're pals. And especially when they're that damn good. What I actually thought was, 'Wow, this kid is fearless, really funny and brutally honest!' as you'll see in his incredibly original memoir, Dead Serious.

If you have any doubt that the best humor comes from deep, dark places, this page-turner will make you a believer. Malone's life journey, which he describes with blinding transparency and unforgiving irony leaves you laughing your ass off as he candidly exposes how he himself has risen from the bowels of depression and self-loathing to personal and professional success. He does this by sharing intimate stories and biting observations about family, love, and loss. He's got the courage to let you into that sacred cavern of dread that few comics allow mere mortals to go, and you get to see 'how the sausage is made' my friends.

As this world starts to let its guard down in regards to recognizing and dealing with mental health issues, books like this become more relevant and relatable than ever. Pepper in some blatant honesty, wickedly funny stories, and the lessons of attempting to love yourself while losing those you love, and you'll discover why Dead Serious is a stand-alone victory mirroring what we need most in today's fractured society: healing through humor. And most importantly, hope.

This book is dedicated to my mother, Nancy, and my step-father, Wayne, who raised me with lots of love and humor.

I miss you.

PREFACE

In the past five years, I've lost four grandparents, three uncles, two aunts, three cousins, five classmates, and my parents. I even had a car die on me.

In my lifetime, I've been to over a dozen funerals and only three weddings. Two of those weddings were for the same friend. Luckily for me, I grew up to be a stand-up comedian. My entire job revolves around shedding light on dark topics.

This book is a look inside my mind and my journal since losing my parents. It is a collection of personal stories, random thoughts, and illustrated jokes from life's ups, downs, and in-betweens. Enjoy :-)

CONTENTS

Swimming in Circles	16
Tigers and Tears	33
Tomorrow is Thursday	54
Cold as March	78
Heavenlution	100
Let Them Eat Cake	120
Medium Size Talk	140
Forever June	156
My Haunted Holidays	174
One Last Pinterest Project	185
Luke Warm Water	197

LIFE IS NOT ONE THING.
IT IS AN UNEVEN
MIXTURE OF EXPERIENCES.
LIFE IS TAKING YOUR
SLURPEE CUP FROM THE
7-11 AND FILLING IT WITH
ALL OF THE FLAVORS.

LIFE IS A SUICIDE.

BAD NEWS: BOTH OF MY PARENTS ARE DEAD.

GOOD NEWS: I CAN STAY UP AS LATE AS I WANT NOW.

SOMETIMES THE AUTOCORRECT ON MY PHONE WILL CHANGE THE WORD GPS TO "GOD" AND I NEVER CORRECT IT.

"HEY GARY, GOD SAYS I'LL BE THERE AT 3:30PM."

9/22/18

I am so broken. I keep waiting to feel better, but I honestly don't know if I'll ever be able to piece myself back together.

Humpty Dumpty had a great fall. Then he laid in bed and binge-watched The Office for days on end, eating ice cream and feeling sorry for himself.

All of the King's men tried to put him back together again but they couldn't, because - duh - only you can fix you.

Wait, was Humpty Dumpty about depression? Maybe a suicidal egg?

For the record, I am not a suicidal egg. I have just had a great fall.

APPROXIMATELY 100 ~~PEOPLE~~ DIE EACH YEAR FROM GETTING STEPPED ON BY A COW.

↖ FUCKING IDIOTS

SWIMMING IN CIRCLES

I discovered Mac Miller's "Swimming" album when I felt like I was drowning. I had never been a fan of his before. I didn't dislike him; I just never paid attention to what he was creating. However, my best friend had been an avid Easy Mac fan for years. He was the one who turned me on to the album when it came out in August of 2018.

I lost my parents a few years before, and my fiancé and I had split up at the beginning of that year. I was living all alone in a small studio apartment in the bowels of Hollywood. More importantly, it was the first time I had been left alone with all of my unattended feelings of heartache and grief.

That whole summer, waves of depression crashed over me.

I had grown accustomed to a familiar numbness. I lived in a haze of marijuana while consistently being mocked by the "Are You Still Watching" text splattered across my TV screen.

Of course, I was still watching. I had planned to lay there 'til I died or evaporated or somehow magically got better.

Spoiler alert: None of those things happened.

I consider myself quite lucky that weed is my drug of choice. If I were a drinker, I'd be dead for sure.

Towards the middle of June, right after my dead mother's birthday, I started seeking out therapy for the first time in my life. I grew up in a small town in Ohio, where therapy was something that only real wackos and wealthy people in big Hollywood movies did.

If you try and tell someone in the Midwest that you feel sad, they will laugh and respond, "We're all sad! Now get back to work!"

I grew up in a "tears are for queers" type of town where men were only allowed to show one emotion; Unbridled rage.

Without any prior experience of what to do with my mismanaged emotions, I took it upon myself and started reading a ton of self-help books. I got sober-ish and bought a bicycle. Slowly but surely, I was becoming a citizen of the world again.

After I began to feel a little better, my tour started back up, and suddenly I was put in charge of other people's happiness. Fuck.

"Well, everybody gather 'round,
I'm still standing, sit down,
And I know I've been out,
But now I'm back in town..."

There it was. The chorus that woke me up. I connected with those lyrics more than with any other song I'd ever heard before.

"I know I've been out, but now I'm back in town..."

Wow. I loved the self-awareness of that line.

"Who is this?" I asked my friend.

"This is off of Mac Miller's new album," he responded.

"Mac Miller? Hmm, I don't really fuck with him," I confessed.

That afternoon, I devoured the rest of Mac Miller's "Swimming" album. Twice. It was like he spoke directly to me, and what he said was this; It gets better.

"Somehow we gotta find a way,
No matter how many miles it takes..."

He was going through so much turmoil. He felt like the underdog in his career. He was suffering from addiction. He was heartbroken. Fuck, he was just that; broken.

So was I.

"I was diggin' me a hole,
 big enough to bury my soul,
Weight of the world,
I gotta carry on my own..."

I connected with the album as a fellow artist and as a human. I thought that if he could get better, so could I.

From there, I did a deep dive into his music catalog. I listened to live recordings, mixtapes, Spotify playlists. I became obsessed. I couldn't get enough.

A month later, in September of 2018, Mac Miller - my new guru - died of an accidental overdose. I couldn't wrap my mind around it.

But... but... he was doing so well. He was "better". He was more than better; he was a survivor. He was on the other side of it all. How could this be possible?

"Don't you know that sunshine don't feel right,
When you inside all day,
I wish it was nice out,

But it looked like rain,
Grey skies and I'm drifting, not living forever,
They told me it only gets better...
I'll do anything for a way out of my head..."

Even though Mac didn't make it, I was determined to stay on my path of mental wellness. It wasn't easy, and there were a ton of setbacks. Like the weekend I spent on tour in Little Rock, confined to my hotel bed, surrounded by empty Ben & Jerry's containers and used up rolling-papers. I would only leave my tousled blankets to perform, and then I would retreat to bed as soon as my show was over.

The "Swimming" album soon became my extended theme song. I thought, "If Mac could be vulnerable and raw about his depression, so can I."

I started sharing my story with my audiences, and for the first time in my career, I stopped killing and started connecting. My message was simple; It gets better.

So often, we think that we are the only ones

experiencing whatever the fuck we're experiencing. That's not only dumb, but it's wrong - way wrong. I felt that way for a long time. I thought nobody could be hurting like I was, and I was wrong.

If you're hurting, depressed, or broken, just know that you are not alone. Help is out there and available, even when it doesn't feel like it is.

"Grey skies and I'm drifting,
not living forever,
They told me it only gets better..."

Mac Miller's posthumous album, "Circles", came out at midnight on January 17th, 2020, and it's the first time I've ever stayed awake and waited for a release.

I was so excited to hear the finished thoughts of "Swimming", and it didn't disappoint.

For a few fleeting moments, I felt as though I had my guru back. The songs played as if they were missing pages in my guidebook.

"I spent the whole day in my head,
Do a little spring cleaning,
I'm always too busy dreaming,
Well, maybe I should wake up instead,
A lot of things I regret,
but I just say I forget,
Why can't it just be easy?
Why does everybody need me to stay?
Oh, I hate the feeling,
When you're high but you're underneath the ceiling,
Got the cards in my hand I hate dealing..."

Thank you, Malcolm, for one last life lesson. "Circles" is such a beautiful continuation of his journey and his quest for transparent pain and wellness.

Now rest east, Easy Mac with the cheesy raps. Leaving us all asking, "Who the fuck is Mac Miller?"

KEEP SWIMMING

YOU'RE ON A GOOD HIKE
WHEN YOU STOP AND THINK,
"WHERE AM I?"

YOU'RE ON A GREAT HIKE
WHEN YOU STOP AND THINK,
"WHO AM I?"

DOG: WHAT WAS THAT?

ME: WHAT?

DOG: THAT THING YOU JUST DID ON MY FOREHEAD. IT WAS LIKE A BITE ONLY WITHOUT USING YOUR TEETH.

ME: IT'S CALLED A KISS.

DOG: WHAT'S IT FOR?

ME: TO SHOW AFFECTION. I LOVE YOU.

DOG: I GOTTA BE HONEST, I WISH YOU WOULD HAVE BITTEN ME.

I DIDN'T WANT TO ADMIT I WAS DEPRESSED. IT SEEMED TOO TRENDY.

I feel like 2019 was a big year for anxiety and depression. It seemed like everyone on my Twitter feed was suffering from it. Posting jokes about killing yourself became the popular thing to do. It was fucking gross. I was depressed and I did want to kill myself some days, but I felt like I was devaluing the illness, or being disrespectful to the people who I felt were actually suffering from depression. So I kept my mouth shut.

I eventually got in to see a therapist. It took my health insurance two and a half months before I got to see a doctor — just one of the perks of living in a big city like Los Angeles.

She asked me the standard stuff about my family history and how I was feeling. I told her everybody was dead and the woman I thought I was going to spend the rest of my life with lived in New York now with our dog.

She asked me a few more questions, mostly about stand up and traveling. I confessed to her that over the weekend, I was on tour in Oklahoma, and I spent most of my time in bed. I only got up to eat, shower, and do my shows.

"I think you are suffering from depression." She replied.

"I'm not depressed." I responded, almost laughing.

She pressed me on why I thought I wasn't depressed, and when I couldn't give her an adequate answer, she had me describe what depression looked like to me.

"I don't know... People that are depressed just like lay in bed all day. They have no motivation to do anything. They just sleep and eat. It's like they're trapped in a sinkhole that nobody else can see." I said.

"And tell me about your weekend in Oklahoma again." She cunningly responded.

"Fuck. I am depressed." I replied in defeat.

EVERY LIFE HAS A STORY, MAKE YOURS A MURDER MYSTERY.

"MAN, THIS FEELS LIKE THE GREAT DEPRESSION."

"WOW, ITS NOT THAT BAD."

"OH, SORRY... I WAS TALKING ABOUT ME."

6/14/18

I am not well,
I am not okay,
I am falling apart,
Piece by piece,
Day by day.

TIGERS & TEARS

I was on a routine phone call with my aunt a few weeks ago when she shared a story about my mother that I hadn't heard before.

They had gone dress shopping for her upcoming wedding to my step-father, Wayne. My mother came out in a stunning gown, paraded around the mirror, smiling as she took in the dress for all its beauty. She gazed at the sequined dress for a few moments before her smile faded. My mother's gaze turned to glare as she pointed at her reflection and started singing, "Look at that fat sewer rat."

My aunt argued with her about the fit of the dress and reassured her that she looked incredible. My mother continued to sing, "Look at that fat sewer rat," over and over before disappearing back into the changing room.

My mother loved to shop. Well, out of magazines, mostly. I don't know why my mother enjoyed it so much. She never kept any of it. A blouse or a nice pair of pants would arrive in the mail. She would try them on and complain about how they made her stomach stick out or how fat her legs looked and then seal them up and ship them back.

My mother was beautiful, and all of the clothes she ordered looked fine. She didn't hate the clothes. She hated her body — another great trait that I inherited from my parent's gene pool: Body image issues.

I was overweight for most of my childhood, and whenever I tell someone that they always ask me the same thing. "How fat were you?" I don't remember a number, but I do remember being "such a great friend" to all the girls I had a crush on in my grade.

I was so big they recruited me to play Center on the football team in high school. In case you're not sports savvy, the whole goal of that position is to be a giant wall to help block the Quarterback. It's an important job, but not a hard one. It requires zero athleticism. You don't even have to remember any plays. Your entire job is to lift your head up and block. That's it. That way, the Quarterback has time to throw the ball and fingerbang that girl you have a crush on.

After high school, I dropped most of my extra weight but somehow managed to continue to carry the body image issues with me. And just like my mother, I enjoy shopping via mail. I'll order some things online, try them on, complain about how they make me look, and then ship them back.

The only place my mother enjoyed shopping in real life was Kohls. If Kohls cash were real, my mother would have been a multi-millionaire. Every time I would visit her, we would head to Kohls so she could score me an extra twenty-five percent off socks or cologne. It made her feel good, and making her feel good made me feel good. So fuck It - hand over the Star Wars -

-themed socks.

She would pick out God awful graphic t-shirts that were stained with items from my childhood.

"I thought you liked the Ninja Turtles?" She'd ask after I turned her suggestion down.

"I do... but that has a crew neck, it's bright green, and it feels like it's made of solid oak wood," I'd explain.

My mother would have made an awful personal shopper. The problem was that once she learned about something you liked, that became the theme for the rest of your life.

My mother was a very generous person. She would shower you with endless amounts of gifts on holidays and birthdays, all sharing the same theme that you had casually mentioned once in a passing conversation.

My mother once asked me what my favorite animal was, and without thinking too hard, I claimed "Tigers." The next thing I knew, my bedspread was tiger print. The curtains, throw pillows, accent rugs, were all tiger! Even my fucking nightstand was a three-foot ceramic tiger standing on its four legs with its back hunched over flat so you could place a lamp on it. And yeah, the lamp too.

My bedroom looked like the clearance section of a ROSS. But again, it made her feel good, and making her feel good made me feel good. So fuck it-hand over the tiger print wastebasket.

Last year, I was on tour in Texas, and I was staying with my best friend in between my shows. He had to run some errands one afternoon and make a few returns, so I tagged along.

After about twenty minutes of driving, we arrived at one of the biggest Kohls I have ever seen. It made a Super Walmart look like a mall kiosk. It had an escalator on the inside. Yeah, that's right -I said this Kohls had a fucking escalator on the inside! And look, I know everything is bigger in Texas, but this was ridiculous.

He ditched me somewhere near the electronic

backscratchers and men's shoe section and took the escalator up to Heaven, I assume. I walked around aimlessly for a few minutes before arriving in the young men's part of the obese store. I could feel the cool breeze of the air conditioning wisp through my hair as a vintage nineties pop playlist played overhead.

Suddenly memories of all the afternoons I spent there with my mother started flooding my haunted psyche. Kohls was one of the last places I went with my mother and just two days before she died. I hate that, but it's true. It's also where I bought my dress shoes for her funeral. And with some of her leftover Kohls cash too.

I hope nobody rats me out for using my dead mother's Kohls cash. I'm not real clear on what the statute of limitations on something like that is, but it's only been a few years.

I couldn't help it. I started to cry and cry hard. I'm talking about "got dumped on your prom night" kind of cries. I was sobbing next to a rack of Avenger's t-shirts and the Ninja blenders.

I tried to muffle the sound, but this Kohls was so cavernous that my bellowing cries echoed past housewares and reached across into the expecting mothers' section.

My friend found me as I was wrapping up my uncontrollable tantrum and confronted me with concern, "Are you fucking crying at a Kohls?"

After that episode, I started making dates with my depression, so it doesn't spring up on me like that again.

Around the holidays, I make time to be sad. I wait until I can be alone and dig out some old photographs or home movies. I play music that purposely hits me in the feels. I embrace my emotions, and I sulk.

Every year I play a voicemail of my mother saying, "Happy birthday, bud. I miss you." I listen to it over and over again, and I cry and cry. That way, at least I feel like I have some control over those emotions instead of being randomly overtaken by them. Because let's be honest, nobody wants to be the guy that's crying at a fucking Kohls.

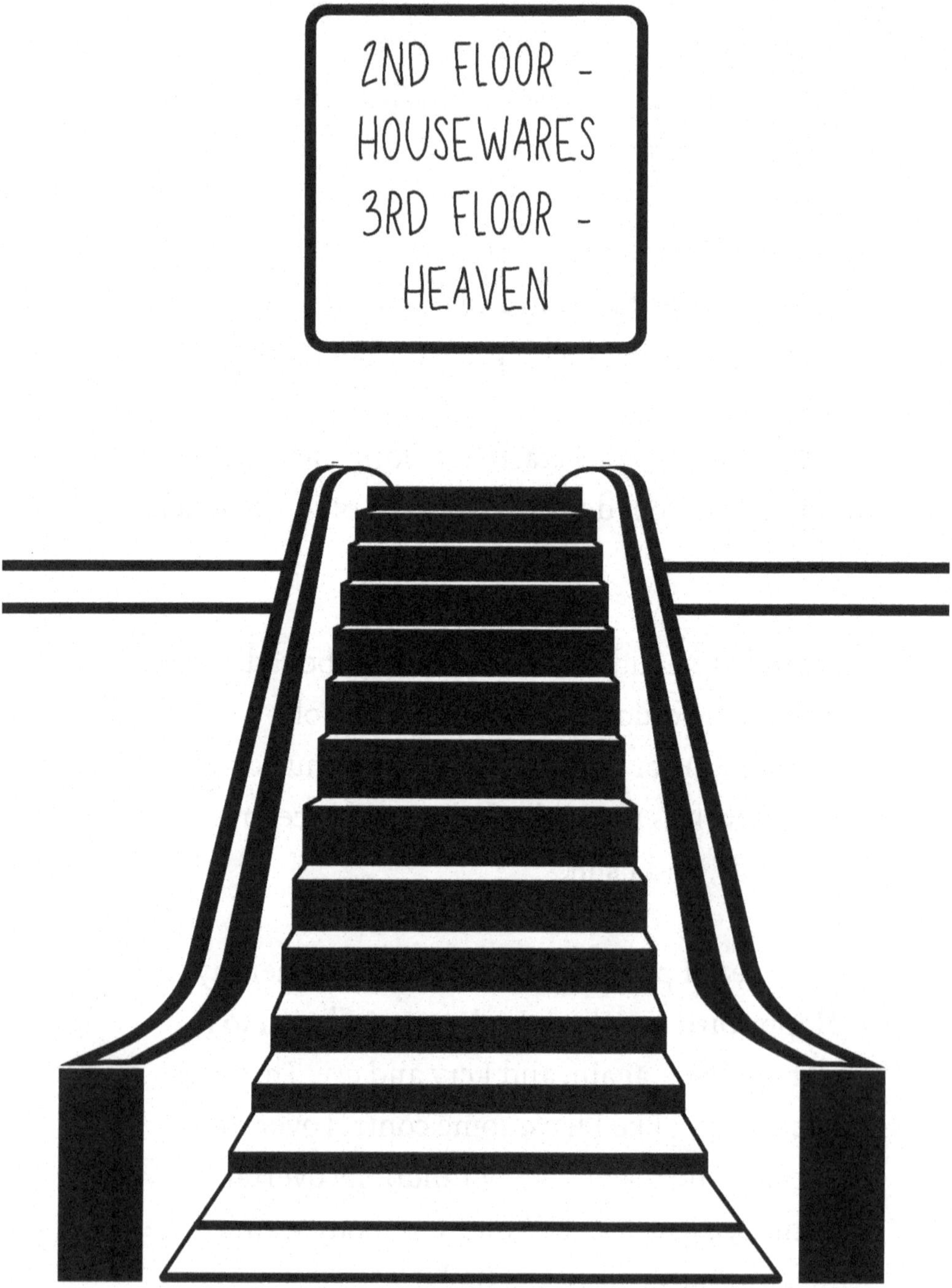
2ND FLOOR -
HOUSEWARES
3RD FLOOR -
HEAVEN

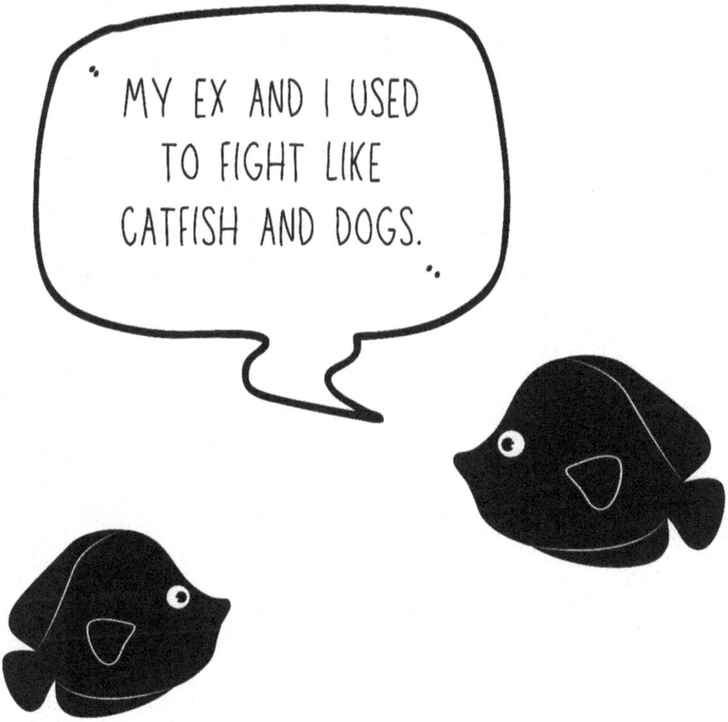
MY EX AND I USED TO FIGHT LIKE CATFISH AND DOGS.

GOODBUY KROOL WURLD.

SUICIDE NOTE FROM A TERRIBLE SPELLER

8/12/16

After we finished cleaning out my mother's house, my grandmother came over to say goodbye to the place. Neither one of us had any intentions of ever stepping foot in that house again.

Even now, when I think of my mother's home, nothing has moved. Everything is just how she left it. There is plenty of apple pie and sweet tea for the taking.

My grandmother and I stood in the kitchen, gazing into the now barren home. After a few minutes of silence, she spoke;

"Empty house, empty hearts."

CAN YOU FEEL LONELY WHEN YOU'RE AROUND A GROUP OF PEOPLE?

SHORT ANSWER: YES.
LONG ANSWER: FUCK YEAH, DUDE!

The feeling of loneliness has very little to do with your surroundings and a lot more to do with connection. It is the lack of reciprocity that triggers loneliness.

I have been in rooms filled with hundreds of people before and have felt alone. It's not their fault either. Sometimes, I have nothing to offer to the conversations. I end up in my head battling anxious thoughts on an endless loop until I finally just shut everything off.

When everything goes silent, that's when loneliness comes in like a desperate, thrice-divorced father of two, buying one last shot before close.

Of course, I'm going to go home with him, because there's nothing else to do. Loneliness is the only thing at the bar that wants to fuck me.

I am so desperate for a connection that I mistake it for love.

THERAPIST OFFICE: BEFORE WE CAN SEE YOU, I HAVE TO ASK YOU A FEW QUESTIONS.

ME: OKAY...

THERAPIST OFFICE: ARE YOU SUICIDAL?

ME: NO.

THERAPIST OFFICE: ARE YOU A HARM TO OTHERS?

ME: NO.

THERAPIST OFFICE: DO YOU HAVE A DRUG OR ALCOHOL ABUSE PROBLEM?

ME: NO.

THERAPIST OFFICE: ... WHY ARE YOU CALLING?

I HAVE A FRIEND WHO IS SUPER RELIGIOUS. HE DOESN'T BELIEVE THAT I AM AN ATHEIST.

I TOLD HIM TO HAVE FAITH.

I FEEL LIKE THE IDEA OF "WHAT'S NEXT" IS ONE OF THE BIGGEST CAUSES OF DEPRESSION.

The process of schooling alone is stressful. You go from kindergarten to grade school. From there to high school. From high school to college and from college to a career. The constant pressure of achieving and progressing makes it impossible to be present and happy in the moments of now.

After you graduate, it's a whole new ball game. You find yourself becoming overwhelmed with keeping up with your peers. You start asking yourself, "How much time do I have left?" Or worse, "What goals have I completed that society has set for me?" and "Why can't I hit those goals like everyone else?"

Finally, you give up.

It's essential to take the time and acknowledge the progress that you have already made. Nobody else is going to do it. It has to be you. Self-praise is a necessity in the journey of life, and it is crucial in the mission of mental wellness.

My girlfriend and I like to hike a mountain down the road from us here in California. It's a tough hike. It's around one-hundred and thirty flights of stairs, according to her Apple Watch.

We go at different times of the day and year, so sometimes it's ninety-something degrees and sunny, and those days it's stupid hard to climb.

No matter what the weather is like I want to give up about halfway every time we go.

However, the last time we went, I did something different. After we got over the initial hard part and there was a little flat land before the last part of the climb, I stopped and celebrated.

I celebrated getting over the hard part to motivate me to keep climbing. You have to stop and celebrate and be present and happy in those moments of achievement, or else you'll feel like giving up.

You have to be your own cheerleader, coach, and player in life.

Stop beating yourself up over the things that you haven't accomplished yet, and celebrate the progress you've already made.

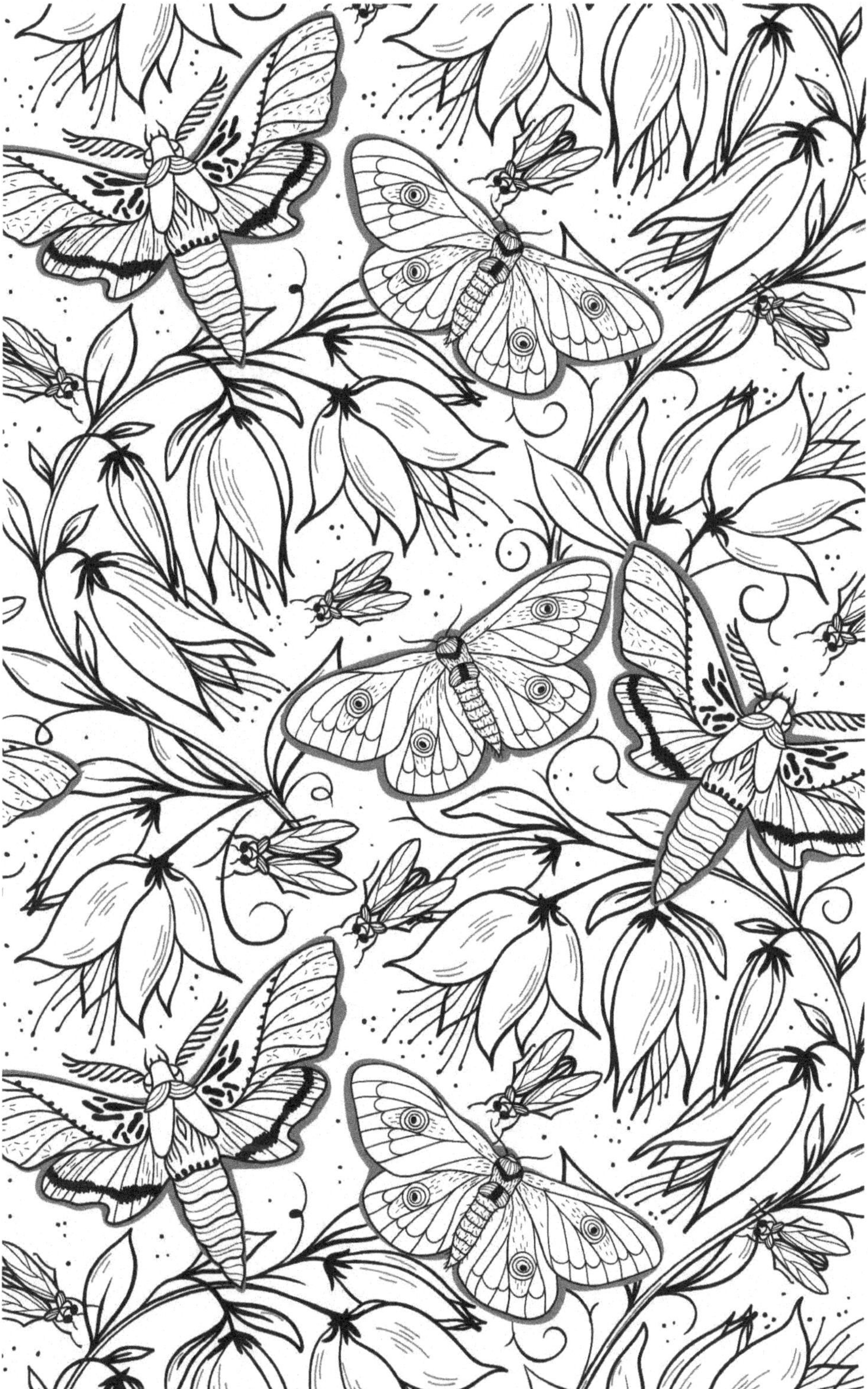

5/14/17

I keep my sober moments brief because that is when your memory haunts me the most.

SELF-HELP WANTED

APPLY WITHIN

TOMORROW IS THURSDAY

"Be in the moment. Clear your mind and be in this moment," were the words that played on an endless loop in my mind.

This was a new exercise I was trying out. The goal was to quiet my thoughts. Be present. That way I could focus my energy on capturing moments. I discovered it in one of those quirky self-help books that line the back wall of the novelty section in those stores that sell forty dollar graphic t-shirts at the mall. I was skeptical but desperate.

I'm not good at letting my mind rest, and I'm fucking terrible at capturing moments.

Some people have what is known as a "photographic memory". Mine works more like Snapchat. I hold on to information for about seven seconds, and then it's gone forever.

I was sitting in an uncomfortable hospital chair, gazing out of a small window, that overlooked an autumn-colored treeline, attached to an empty parking lot.

I could barely hear my grandmother's fragile voice over the phrase, "Be in the moment," which was on 'scream-peat' in my mind.

My grandmother is ninety-two years of age and full of two things: shit and vinegar. Despite her age, she was both sharp as a whip and ornery as hell.

She had recently fallen on her back porch and broke her elbow, so her left arm was in a cast. She fell again a few weeks after that and sprained her right wrist. Because you know, grandmas be tripp'in.

She had both arms completely wrapped up

in bandages. They just flapped around at her sides like a drunk penguin. Watching her eat lunch was equal parts heartbreaking and hilarious.

She would hold her fork with one hand, steady it with the other, bend forward as far as she could, and sort of flip food into her mouth. She had the accuracy of a young Shaquille O'Neal at the free-throw line.

It was hard to watch, but my grandmother was stubborn and refused any help whatsoever. At one point, I made the mistake of scooting her pudding cup two inches closer to her seal-like grip, and she screamed at me, "You trying to feed me like a baby!?!"

"No," I nervously responded. "I just wanted to help."

She pointed her head down like a bull, and in a low tone, she growled back at me, "I don't need anyone's help. I'm fine."

My grandmother then proceeded to clap her hands together in a sloppy attempt to pick up her spoon. It slid across her slick plastic food tray like an air hockey puck. Banking off the side railings for a few moments before she cornered it, scooped up some pudding with it, and then tossed the food towards her hunched and widened mouth.

It was also hard to watch because, even though my grandmother is in her early nineties - Well, there's nothing really "early" about your nineties. Anyways, even though she was older, she was still very active, and I don't mean like, "she still walks out to get her newspaper in the yard" active. I mean, the woman will "fight you over a shovel in the middle of winter" active.

I can still hear her voice cutting through the frost, "I'm going to shovel my driveway, and if I die doing it, then I die doing it! Now, go inside!"

They say you should never meet your heroes, but I'd argue it's worse to watch them get old. I prefer to meet Batman and find out he's a dick than watch him groan as he uses a shoehorn to put on his Bat Boots in the morning.

"I'm going home tomorrow," my grandmother said with a grin.

"Is that what the doctor said? You could go home?" I responded loudly, so her old ears could pick up my response.

"Yes. The doctor said I could go home," she repeated, with even more excitement.

"I think he said you could go to 'a home', not 'your home', I replied with a chuckle.

"I'm not going to a nursing home -- I'm going home!" My grandmother erupted.

"You're not going home," I calmly rebutted.

"Why not?" She asked firmly.

"Because you got no fucking arms!" I said.

"I have arms! I don't have hands -- but I got arms!" She spit back at me.

"Even worse!" I argued.

Her roommate chimed in from the other side of the closed curtain, "The doctor said she needs to be in a nursing home."

My grandmother leaned in close to my face, and with a fiery whisper, she said, "I'm going to smother her."

We sat in silence for a few moments after our exchange.

Well, it wasn't silent for me. I was still repeating my new mantra in my head.

"Be. In. The. Moment." I repeated.

"I've thought about throwing myself down my basement steps," my grandmother confessed. "I don't know why I'm still here. I don't know why He won't take me already." She continued.

What a sad and haunting thought. Forced existence.

My grandmother has a pacemaker and a defibrillator, so whether she wants to or not, she's waking up in the morning. Every morning. She couldn't die even if she tried.

Last December, she was in hospice care. After a week, the doctor came to us and said, "We think your grandmother can go home now."

We thought he meant like, "Home, home," Ya' know? Where Grandpa and my turtle that died in the sixth grade live. "Home".

Nope. It turns out; he did mean her own house. My grandmother is part of the rare 12% of people that survive after being in hospice care.

She is also one of the only two children left alive out of nine other siblings. Her husband passed away back in 1994, and two out of her three children have also died.

About a year ago, she had a hip replacement. The summer before that, her knee got knocked out of place. She had colon cancer last year for one week. Yes, one week. Then she had it surgically removed and went back to normal life. I've had more issues dealing with cavities in my teeth than my grandmother had with colon cancer.

But she wasn't so lucky this time. This time, she was sitting in a hospital bed with two barely usable arms and pudding stains all over the front of her gown.

So, I didn't blame her. I'd want to throw myself down a set of stairs too if I were her.

"I fell out of bed, and I couldn't get up," she began to tell me.

"Yeah, I've seen that commercial," I interrupted.

She laughed. "No, no, I'm serious. I just laid there for a few minutes, wondering if I was going to die. And when I didn't die, I decided to crawl to the kitchen," she continued.

"What -- crawl to the kitchen?! Were you planning on making a sandwich before calling Life Alert?" I anxiously asked.

"I scooted to the kitchen on my back," she said as she began to wiggle around in her squeaky hospital bed. "I thought, if I got to the kitchen, I could pull myself up on one of the countertops," she continued.

"You got no fucking arms!" I exclaimed.

She let out a laugh and then sank her head in defeat. "I hate it here," my grandmother murmured just loud enough for Jesus to hear.

"I keep calling Mary by your mother's name. I know she hates it. She probably hates me. I don't mean to do it. I just miss Nancy," she confessed.

My mother, Nancy, and she were close. They were more like sisters than they were mother and daughter. My grandmother was actually with my mother the night she died. She carries a lot of guilt with her about that night.

My mother had gotten sick and was having trouble sleeping. So most nights, my grandmother would sit on the hard, living room floor while my mother laid on the couch. They would comment back and forth on lousy reality television shows, and my grandmother would pet my mother's large Bernese mountain dog, Saddie, until all three of them would drift off.

The night my mother died, my grandmother woke up sore from dozing off on the hardened floor and left my mother to finish sleeping on the couch, like she had done many nights before. Early the next morning, my grandmother went over to check on my mother and found her daughter lifeless and pale lying on the sofa.

Guilt like that stains your soul. It's hard to get rid of because guilt like that is attached to a math problem that can never be solved.

"What if she would have stayed with her that night?"

"What if she would have checked on her sooner?"

"What if my mother called out, but she couldn't hear her, because she was left alone in her time of need?"

"What if... What if... What if..."

Forgiveness for something like that has to come from within yourself. It's not something any doctor, therapist, or carpenter can give you. I don't care who His Father claims to be.

"Fuck - stop! Be in the moment. Clear your mind, and just be in this moment..." I scolded myself mentally.

Just when I regained my focus, my grandmother's voice broke through my fragile mantra.

"Tomorrow is Thursday, right?" She asked.

"Yes, tomorrow is Thursday," I replied.

My grandmother's face got long, and she looked towards the window, hoping to hide her tears.

"You leave on Thursday," she said with a deep sadness.

I put my hands on hers. Well, her good hand. Well, the one with fewer bandages on it. Honestly, it felt like I was holding hands with Fire Marshall Bill. I gripped her wrinkly and torn skin as the light texturing of ACE bandage covered my palm.

"I'll be back soon," I reassured her. "But for now, let's just be in this moment. What do you say?"

"Okay," she responded with a smile. "I could sit with you in this moment forever. I love you, honey. More than you'll ever know," she continued, fighting back more tears.

We sat in silence for a few brief moments before her roommate's voice came crashing through the curtain, "Did you hear me? The doctor said she needs to be in a nursing home."

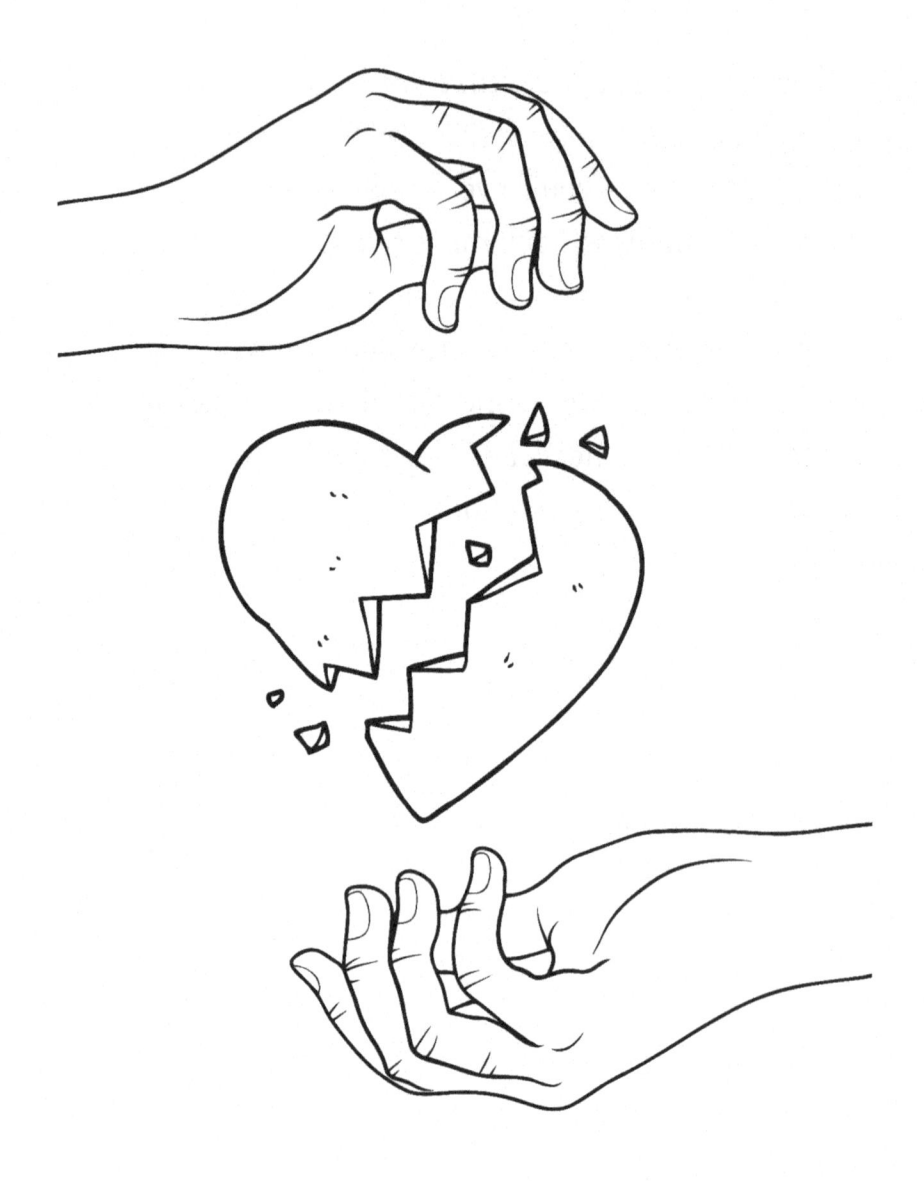

ME: WHO'S A GOOD BOY?

DOG: IS IT ME?! IS IT ME?!!

ME: YES! YOU ARE A GOOD BOY!

DOG: THEN WHY DIDN'T YOU JUST SAY THAT?

ME: WHAT?

DOG: WHY DIDN'T YOU JUST SAY IT INSTEAD OF HAVING ME GUESS? YOU ALMOST GAVE ME A PANIC ATTACK.

ME: I JUST--

DOG: NAH, DICK MOVE.

SHARKS KILL FEWER THAN
10 PEOPLE PER YEAR.
ACCORDING TO A STUDY
DONE ENTIRELY BY SHARKS.

5/14/17

Even though my mother is gone, she is still able to teach me humility and empathy.

I see her face, her spirit, and principals in so many people in my travels.

Their actions reflect and remind me of my mother, and I find myself mimicking them as if following in the same steps that she laid out in front of me.

YOU SHOULD BE COMPARING YOURSELF AGAINST YOURSELF AND ONLY YOURSELF.

It's easy to get distracted by the presentation of others via social media. You ever see someone's post on Instagram, and they are reading a book at the beach with their ass hanging out? They have their morning coffee, and the sun is hitting them just perfectly, and they are glowing. You sit there and stare at their photo and think, "Fuck, I wish that was my life."

Well, the good news is, that's not their real-life either. It is merely a snap-shot of what their day was that day.

You are drooling over a small moment of what might be a cluster fuck of a life.

You have to remember that you are only seeing that little piece, of that little day, of that little year of that little life.

It doesn't matter how nice their car is or how many abs they have. It is foolish to allow yourself to get hung up on envy.

You can not compare the outside of others to the inside of you. All you can do is work on getting better on the inside. Learning to love yourself and getting stronger mentally, because the better you feel about yourself, the less all those other things will matter.

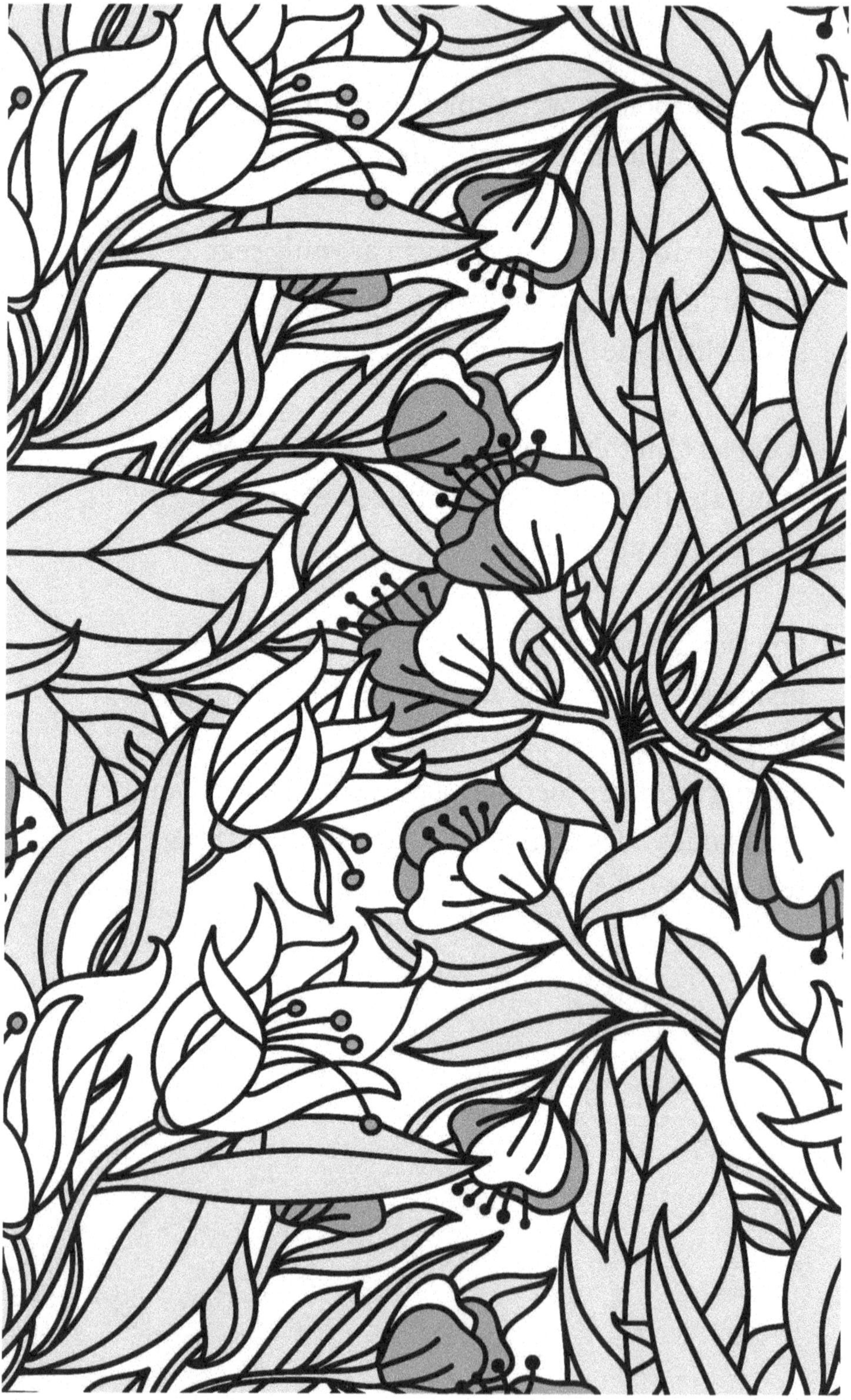

I GREW UP IN THE MIDWEST, WHERE EVERYONE IS TOLD THEY ARE NOT IMPORTANT, AND THEN I MOVED TO LOS ANGELES, WHERE EVERYONE IS TOLD THEY ARE SUPER IMPORTANT. PEOPLE FROM THE MIDWEST ARE NOT POLITE. WE JUST WEREN'T RAISED WITH ANY SELF-WORTH.

SO YEAH, OF COURSE, I'LL HOLD THE DOOR OPEN FOR YOU. I AM TRASH.

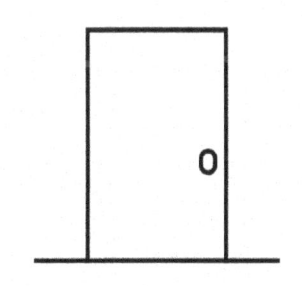

I NEVER MASTURBATE IN THE SHOWER. I DON'T THINK IT'S GROSS OR ANYTHING, I JUST CAN'T GET THE SHOWER HOSE AROUND MY NECK TIGHT ENOUGH.

THE AUDITIONING WORLD IS VERY SIMILAR TO THE DATING WORLD. YOU HEAR THE SAME THINGS...

"THEY LOVED YOU!"

"REALLY GREAT CHEMISTRY."

"SORRY, THEY ENDED UP GOING WITH A BLACK GUY."

2/26/19

This might be my last year in LA.

Why am I still here? Ego?

What am I doing here? Nothing.

Am I scared? Bored? Not good enough? Bitter? Probably all of the above.

Why am I still here? Ego?

I am not auditioning. I am not performing. I am just existing here. I am not growing. I am not working. I am not taking advantage of this city at all.

Why am I still here? Ego?

KEEP SWIMMING

KEEP SWIMMING

KEEP SWIMMING

KEEP SWIMMING

KEEP SWIMMING

KEEP SWIMMING

COLD AS MARCH

My mother always went out of her way to hide the ugliness of my father's alcoholism, addiction, and random drug use from me in hopes of preserving his image. She didn't share a whole lot about him in general with me either. People on dating apps know more about complete strangers than I do about my own father.

Once, on holiday, my mother and I were riding in the car when she casually pointed out the passenger side window and said, "That's the prison your father went to," as if it were his old alma mater.

I was thirty-one years old when this happened, and I had never heard that story. I still have never heard that story because my mother quickly caught herself and changed the subject.

My father was tall, bald, and confident. He loved watching boxing, playing golf, and listening to Tom Petty.

It's funny. One of my last memories with my father involves Tom Petty. We were both sitting on our brand new and very uncomfortable, yet broad, sectional couch watching the music video for "Last Dance with Mary Jane" just a few weeks before my father's death.

Looking back now, I can't help but think to myself, "How fitting."

My father was part Irish and part Native American, so addiction ran through his veins. I know my father struggled with addiction because he passed some of those lovely genes onto me. I, somehow, have gone thirty-seven years without drinking alcohol.

79

People never believe me, but it's true. Sure, I've tasted alcohol in my life, but I've never consumed more than a gulp.

When I was in high school, my parents went to Tennessee for a weekend, so naturally, I threw a house party in their honor. My friends were reckless, and my house was always the hangout, which made them way too comfortable. They knew where everything of any importance was hidden and didn't mind breaking shit either. We were teenagers. There was not an item that 'my bad' wouldn't magically repair.

That night, they attempted to make oven pizza on my step-father's outdoor grill. I don't know if you have ever tried to do that, but it's a fucking optical illusion. The top of the pizza looks like something you'd see on a TV commercial. It was radiant. It looked as if it were airbrushed. However, the underside was charred beyond recognition and inedible.

I was not in charge of the food that particular night. I was making drinks. I had just made a fresh gallon of purple Kool-Aid, which I was in the process of spiking with half a bottle of Mike's Hard Lemonade.

Yup. That's right. I mixed in one half of one bottle of Mike's Hard Lemonade into a one-gallon jug of grape Kool-Aid, which I then poured into an eight-ounce drinking glass. And that, my friends, is the most alcohol I've ever had in my entire life.

My story is different from my father's, no matter how much my mirror likes to reflect our similarities. I am not anything like my father.

My father drank — a lot.

When I was eleven, we moved into a mid-size two-story country home. During the move I came across a VHS tape that would change my view on the effects of alcohol for the rest of my life.

I pushed play and watched as a fuzzy image of my father came into focus. He was sitting at the dinner table; his eyes were bloodshot and empty. His body hunched over a plate of scrambled eggs.

"Did you go out drinking again last night?" My

mother interrogated from behind a small handheld camcorder.

My father ignored her.

He extended one of his long arms and pulled a paper plate of large open-faced red tomatoes closer to him. He began to cut them into slices with a fork and steak knife, except as he cut into the juicy tomato, he would also cut clean through the paper plate beneath them. Then, with a fork, he would unknowingly bundle up both of the items and, yup, right down the hatch.

"Those tomatoes taste good, Craig?" my mother asked with a devilish smirk.

"They're great," my father answered with a mouthful of paper plate and tomatoes.

I think a lot of the addiction that my father struggled with came after he was in a bad car accident. More people in my family have been hit by vehicles and survived than I can count. My father drove a semi-truck cross-country for a few years before settling down into driving a forklift at one of the factories in my small hometown. The night he got T-boned, the doctor warned us that my father might never be able to walk again.

I remember lying in his hospital bed with him and his lifeless legs. His eyes were bloodshot and empty, just like I had seen on that old VHS tape years later. It was caused by the pain medication the doctor had given him.

This ER doctor became my father's first drug dealer.

My father left the hospital in crutches, and he eventually had full use of both his legs, but those pain pills my father got addicted to would end up killing him one day.

I don't have a lot of memories of my father. He wasn't around for most of my childhood. Don't get me wrong. My father loved children; he just didn't want anything to do with them once they started talking. There are plenty of photographs of my father and me from ages zero to five. After that, you'd be hard-pressed to find any real moments captured between us.

To put it another way, my father loved having kittens around, but he hated owning cats. My mother should have known better. My dad already lacked custody of three other cats from a previous marriage.

My father was on everything but the right path. He kept strange hours and even stranger friends, so he slept on the couch most nights.

It was kind of perfect. My mother and I would stay at home and watch Nickelodeon while my father was out bar hopping. We'd both be in bed long before my father would stumble into our old farmhouse at night.

One night, my mother and I were midway through an episode of Salute Your Shorts when my father came staggering in through the backdoor. I remember smelling him before actually seeing his body darken the living room entry. The only light in the room was coming from the glow on the television. It grimly lit up my father's tall frame that slumped against the wall.

"I need a ride downtown," my father announced.

"Didn't you just come from there?" my mother inquired.

Before my father could answer, my mother, cut him off.

"Craig, where is your car?! How did you get home?" she asked in a panic.

"Relax, Nancy," my father grumbled. "A guy at the bar told me that I was too drunk to drive... and he asked me for my car keys... so I gave them to him, and he called me a cab," he stammered.

"Craig, do you know this man? Was he a friend of yours?" my mother quizzed in anger.

"No - Hell no, I don't know him, but he seemed like a good guy," my father proudly admitted.

I sat in the backseat as my mother drove my father and me a few blocks past the dingy bars downtown just after midnight. We finally arrived in a part of town that looked like it had been forgotten. The grass was overgrown. Porch steps were missing on the frontend of most of the houses. Dogs were chained up outside. Big dogs, too. Some of the biggest dogs I had ever seen, and we owned a Siberian Husky.

"There's my car," my father said as if he had parked it himself.

My mother parked behind it on the crowded street. I could see there were scattered lights on throughout the house we pulled up to because there was no glass in the windows. Some of them just had boards nailed to the openings — some with large black trash bags instead of curtains.

I watched my father walk into this seemingly abandoned house after midnight on a Wednesday evening as if he were casually running into the bank as part of an afternoon errand.

My mother and I both sat in tense silence for what felt like a lifetime. Finally, my father appeared in the dimly lit doorway. He crouched by my mother's driver's side window on the way to his car.

"See ya back at the house," my father blurted out

before almost skipping to his vehicle.

My father wasn't scared of the neighborhood we were currently parked in because he had been there before. This must be where he goes after the bars in town close. I was too young to put it all together back then, but I was aware something was off. This didn't look like a place my other friends' dads would hang out. I never asked either of my parents about that night or any other night like that one. All I can do now is try to put these scattered puzzle pieces together in hopes it shapes an accurate image of who my father was.

People are made of two things; the stories they tell themselves and the stories people tell about them. We, as the observer, can only gain access to the latter.

My father was much more than his addiction. He was a brother, a son, a good father to his other children, a loyal husband, and a Vietnam war veteran.

Much like the frozen pizza, my friends barbecued on my step-father's outdoor grill; perspective is vital. Some people would view my father as a damn near perfect pizza. However, I am left with memories of the underside. Crisp, charred, and hard to digest.

My father passed away in March of 1995, almost a month after I turned twelve years old. It was cold, but the sun was doing that thing it does in Ohio, where it'll come out just enough to give you hope - teasing us in the way only Ohio weather can. The weather in Ohio has Tourette's. It's hot then it's cold. It's snowing; then suddenly, you're on a boat. If it gets above thirty-five degrees in the winter, real Ohioans will grill out.

My mother was making her standard French toast breakfast that morning, which included an ice cream scoop of butter, thick Texas toast style bread, and a gallon and a half of nonfat maple syrup. She had yelled for my father to join us a few times but wasn't getting a response. Not even the usual low hungover grumble.

My mother shouted towards the living room a few more times before sending me to fetch my father for breakfast.

His forehead was ice cold. Colder than any day in March. His body was still, and for once, he looked utterly at peace.

I didn't cry.

I didn't scream.

I didn't move.

I was numb.

Whatever emotions I was feeling at the time were all jammed in my stomach and throat. It felt like the feeling you get in your gut right as the lock bar comes down on top of you on a roller coaster.

Fuck, I hope I survive this.

BREAKFAST REALLY IS THE MOST IMPORTANT MEAL OF THE DAY. MY FATHER MISSED IT ONE TIME - DEAD.

GIRL, I'M LIKE A LATE NIGHT SNACK. AFTER YOU PUT ME IN YOUR MOUTH, I GO STRAIGHT TO YOUR THIGHS AND BUTT.

COMPROMISE FOR GUN LOVING CONSERVATIVES:

ABORTIONS REMAIN LEGAL, BUT THE DOCTOR USES AN AR-15.

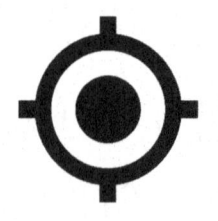

THERE ARE NO RULES.

Most of the things that you are anxious about aren't real. They are just suggestions designed by society.

You don't HAVE to go to college.

You don't HAVE to get married.

You don't HAVE to watch the Super Bowl and drink an ice-cold Pepsi to experience happiness.

Those societal norms they push on you are all man-made. Ask yourself what it is you want out of life, take control, and break some rules because those rules don't belong to anyone.

I RUINED A WHOLE BAG OF WEED AND THREE APPLES THE LAST TIME I WAS IN CANADA.

Somebody gave me a giant bag of weed after one of my shows because I'm hilarious but mainly because Canadians are super friendly. The problem is, I don't know how to roll a joint, so I called my buddy for some guidance.

"Dude, just turn an apple into a pipe," He effortlessly advised. As if that were common knowledge.

It turns out; My friend was right. You take an apple, cut a couple of holes in it. Then you put weed in the top hole and smoke out of the side hole. So I cut a hole here, and there and then...

I just made weed wet.

GET HIGH WITH THIS FUN DIY

HERE

THERE

THERE ARE MORE THAN 10,000 VARIETIES OF TOMATOES. HOWEVER, THE TWO MOST POPULAR ONES ARE TOMAYTO AND TOMAHTO.

THE YOUNGEST POPE WAS
11 YEARS OLD.

HE SUCKED HIS OWN DICK.

MY FATHER & MY DAD

My stepfather, Wayne, took up a role that I don't think my biological father could ever have done even if he had lived past my 12th birthday.

My father and my dad. Two very different men with completely different outlooks, habits, and ways of life.

However, I need the good and the bad parts of both men's past to shape my future. The examples that they have passed onto me run deeper than breakable habits. It's moral identity and guidance. The building blocks to the man I will become.

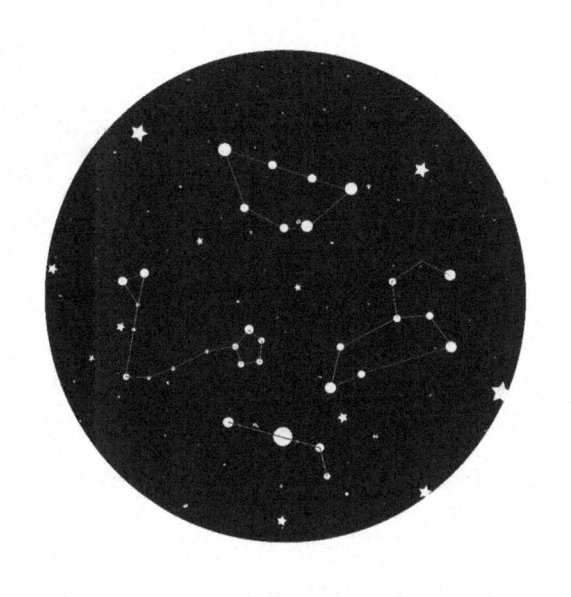

MERCURY HAS NO ATMOSPHERE, WHICH MEANS THERE IS NO WIND OR WEATHER. THAT'S WHAT MAKES IT YOUR GRANDPARENT'S FIRST PICK ON PLACES TO LIVE WHEN THEY RETIRE.

HEAVENLUTION

"You don't believe in evolution?" I shouted. "It's all around you, Mom! Plants, animals, people! You are surrounded by evolution," I continued.

I didn't expect to get as high as I did. I knew better, but I couldn't help myself. I wanted one little hit to make my mother's Midwestern cooking taste better.

I can't smoke at my mother's house. I mean, I'm allowed but I shouldn't. I think most people would agree that you shouldn't smoke pot, fuck, or heavily drink at your mother's house when you visit.

However, I am not in that majority.

It was such a tragic scene, too. I was a thirty-two-year-old full-grown adult hunched over my childhood dresser attempting to roll a joint. I use the term "attempting" because I am terrible at rolling joints. I've tried to learn how to do it a bunch of times, too. I've watched YouTube tutorials. I have even picked up one of those tiny, plastic, steam roller thingies you always see in a smoke shop that collects dust beside the register.

I roll the kind of joint that you light, and then it evaporates immediately like a Harry Potter spell. One puff, and like magic - it's gone.

It's pathetic.

I kept pausing to listen for footsteps; I felt like an outlaw in my own home! Well, my own mother's home! At any moment my mother could come crashing in through my old, wooden bedroom door and ruin my fun. I felt like I was back in high school. Maybe I should go down and smoke in the shower, that's how I hid other shameful things from her when I was young. It might still work.

My mother had asked me not to smoke in the house. She could always tell too; she had the nose of a basset hound.

I had found a way to ignore her request respectfully.

I would crack my bedroom window, spray cologne, hell I'd even light some of mother's fancy twenty-six dollar candles. Pro-tip: Nothing covers up the scent of marijuana like an Apple Pumpkin scented candle from Bed Bath & Beyond.

I was prepared to do anything. Anything, except go outside and suffer in the mid-winter temperatures of Ohio to take one measly hit of shitty, hometown cactus weed before dinner.

As soon as the spark hit, I heard harsh pounding on the thin stairway walls. It was our poor man's intercom system.

POUND. POUND. POUND.

"Michael, dinner is ready," my mother shouted up into our tall and narrow stairway.

There was a brief pause, and then...

"Is that smoke? What did I tell you about doing that in the house?!" She shouted.

My step-father, Wayne, had recently passed, and my mother found herself back in the church pew. She needed it. She needed a sense of belonging. Wayne and my mother were together for almost twenty years. Then one afternoon without any warning, he died. My mother felt ripped off. She felt like Death had made a mistake, and maybe he did. We all know Santa Claus checks his list twice, but we never hear about how closely the Grim Reaper keeps track of his inventory.

My mother needed someone to be mad at. She felt like someone messed up, and now she would like to speak to the manager. The church was right for her. It allowed her to be mad at someone, or something, and scream at the sky.

I am not a religious man. I think belief in the supernatural is well, supernatural.

"We were not monkeys!" My mother screamed.

"I'm not saying we were. No, not us, Mom. Not you and me, no, we have always been human. I'm talking about where we came from," I clarified.

"No, we were never monkeys, Michael. God made us in His image, and He is not a monkey." She argued.

"Maybe He is... or was," I responded.

The way she was so sure that God was real (and not a monkey) sent shivers down my spine. It was clear now; they had gotten to her.

I believe Christianity spreads the same way vampires do. The strongest one will sink its teeth into you. You drink some blood of Christ and then - BOOM - you have a craving, nay - a hunger for the Holy Spirit for the rest of your days.

My mother was never an overly religious woman. No, she had a wild side. She was even in a rock band when she was young. Well, she ran the lights for one. The point is, my mom was fucking cool.

It seems like the older people get, the more

religious they become. It makes sense. It's hard to run away from vampires once you get old. We grow up thinking of our parents as superheroes. Bulletproof, and with the strength of ten men. Then as you get older, you realize just how fragile they are. You get a look behind the curtain and discover that your parents are only two people who are trying to make rent, just like you.

My mother was my best friend. She was also one of the strongest, most independent women I have ever met in my entire life. With that said, if you were to ask me for a third descriptive word about my mother, it would be "terrified". She feared the most mundane things. She was crippled by fear, and it just got worse after Wayne died.

I knew she was scared. I was scared too.

I felt like I couldn't leave her. I could never go back home to Los Angeles. She wouldn't make it on her own.

I began having flashbacks of her giving away different types of technology over the years because "they didn't work right anymore." She'd claim. She could barely navigate her email inbox. She still used a flip phone for God's sake!

My mother and I had an honest and open relationship. We could talk about anything, but not this night. No, this night, we argued passionately about the basic idea of evolution for a solid twenty minutes before I gave in and changed the subject. She got angry about that one as well, and the next one, and the one after that. Her words dripped with venom. They stung. She would swell up like a dog who wanted you to know that it's not safe to come near it. She was hurt. Wounded. The irony was, she was behaving like an animal in the wild. Who, if you remember from my mother's previous adamant arguments, have no relation to us whatsoever.

She was hissing and growling, so no one could ever get close to her again. She was scared that if anyone would get as close as Wayne did and something went wrong, she'd die too.

She never said it out loud, but I saw it in her eyes. My mother was alone. Left behind, and very, very angry about it.

HOWARD BE THY NAME

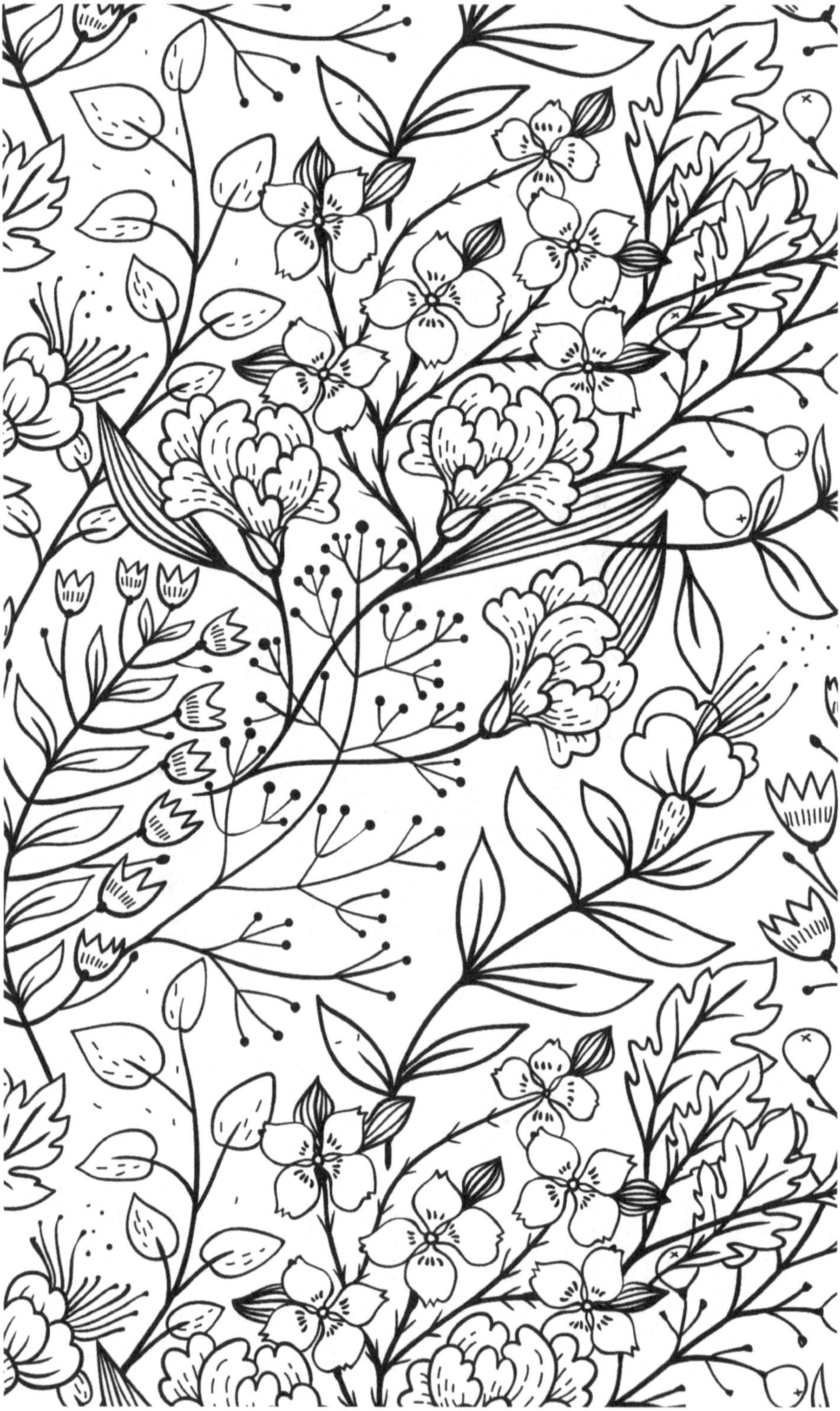

7/08/18

I sat down and journaled for an hour this morning. I can't express how much it helped. I was keeping secrets from myself. I had no idea until I started writing down all the rumblings inside my mind. If you aren't already journaling, you need to start. Make the time. Tell yourself a secret.

ON THE DAYS I CAN'T AFFORD TO SEE A THERAPIST, I HEAD OVER TO MY LOCAL HOME DEPOT AND PICK UP ONE OF THE RANDOM DAY WORKERS WHO ALWAYS STAND OUT FRONT.

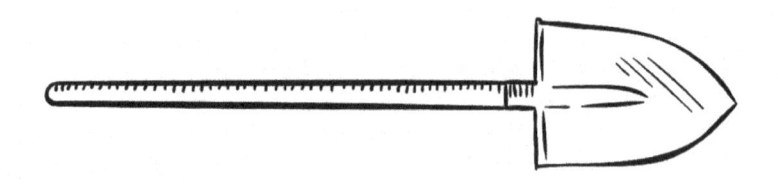

"OH, WE HAVE A LOT OF WORK TO DO... EMOTIONALLY."

DOG: I THINK YOU'RE SMOKING TOO MUCH WEED.

ME: WHAT? WHY DO YOU THINK THAT?

DOG: WELL, YOU THINK I'M TALKING TO YOU RIGHT NOW, RIGHT?

ME: ... FUCK. GOOD POINT.

KETCHUP WAS SOLD IN THE 1830'S AS MEDICINE, AND IT'S STILL CONSIDERED THE BEST CURE FOR MEDIOCRE FOOD TODAY.

MY PARENTS ARE DEAD
AND I AM SINGLE.

MY EMERGENCY
CONTACT NUMBER IS
DOMINO'S PIZZA.

9/13/18

I've only been on dating apps for a couple of months and I'm already exhausted.

This is direct quote from a girl's profile in Texas.

"Not here to date. First and foremost, God is my number one so you will lose."

What a miserable cunt.

After my mother died, I went back to Ohio to clean out her house. On one of my final days there, I discovered a few notes and poems that were addressed to me. They were all hidden inside random books and large picture frames that were hanging on the walls of my mother's old country style home.

Some of which she had written herself, others were poems or thoughts that she had loved and jotted down on napkins and tiny lined notecards so that she could share them with me later.

I feel so grateful to be able to share one of the poems that my mother shared with me. This is my personal favorite and one that I think about quite often. I hope you dig it.

XOXO

Your mother is always with you...

She's the whisper of the leaves as you walk down the street.

She's the smell of certain foods you remember, flowers you pick, the fragrance of life itself.

She's the cold hand on your brow when you're not feeling well,

She's your breath in the air on a cold winters day.

She's the sound of the rain that puts you to sleep,

She's the colors of the rainbow,
She is Christmas morning.

Your mother lives insides your laughter,

She's the place you came from,
Your first home.

She's the map you follow every step you take,

She's your first love, your first friend, even your first enemy.

Nothing on earth can separate you, Not time, Not space, Not even death.

— Anonymous

MY MOTHER LOVED THE HOLIDAYS—ALL OF THEM.

She loved to celebrate the traditions of them with me, especially. It didn't matter how old I got either; I was expected to play along.

The first Easter that I spent living in Los Angeles, my mother called me from back home in Ohio and shouted with excitement, "I hid eggs all over the house! You guess where they are, and I'll tell you if you found one or not!"

I HAD TERRIBLE SEX THE OTHER NIGHT. IT WAS SO BAD; SHE ASKED ME IF I CAME!

LET THEM EAT CAKE

I celebrated most of my childhood birthdays at the local roller skating rink, "The Rolla Roma". I grew up in a town that was too small to hold any secrets, and way too boring to ever be featured on one of those "Top Ten Places to Visit Before Life Itself Skull Fucks You to Death" blogs.

A pair of railroad tracks ran through my backyard. My friends and I would often sneak back and play on them. Oh, and then, of course, there was the largest state prison that this country has ever built, located just on the other side of the tree line, beside those same train tracks on which we would innocently play. It was almost cartoonish. They built a giant prison — no, they built the biggest prison ever built — right next to a large wooded area and train tracks. All that was missing was a big neon sign that read, "Escape Here".

One afternoon, I was playing with a couple of friends on the set of tracks that lined my backyard. Skipping rocks, poking stuff with sticks, talking about boobs, and what we thought cigarettes tasted like — you know, kid stuff — when a cop started walking toward us. He abandoned his car and was heading our way at the speed of a T-1000 from the infamous Terminator movies.

"Ditch those rocks!" I screamed at my friends.

The officer now stood in front of us, his shadow and stern look bearing down on our prepubescent souls. He pulled his oversized aviator sunglasses down onto the bridge of his nose. This was not just a regular police officer. He was from the Highway Patrol. I think I was ten years old at the time, so, to me, the Highway Patrol ranked as high as the FBI.

"And just what in the hell do you kids think you're doing out here on these railroad tracks?" The words slowly poured out of his mouth as if he dipped his anger in molasses.

We were in shock. None of us uttered a single word.

"You kids like Christmas, don't ya?" The officer continued.

"Y-y-yes, sir," I said in a quiver. I was nervous, but I also had a stutter when I was young. I still do sometimes if you catch me off-guard at a restaurant. I know it sounds odd, but I only seem to stutter when I'm ordering food, and the waiter asks me to repeat something. It's almost like my mind is too fast. I'm so far ahead in the conversation that it physically delays me to have to go back and repeat something I said just a few moments earlier. I end up adding seven more "D's" to Diet Coke — or, even worse, I lock up. I look like your screen when you lose a signal during a Facetime call. It's embarrassing.

"Well, you're all going to spend Christmas in that

prison over there if I ever catch you playing on these train tracks again. Understood?" He questioned. "Now, get on outta here!"

We ran back to my house, and none of us ever went near those train tracks again.

After we abandoned playing on train tracks and shooting at bird's nests with my small pellet gun, roller skating at the locally famed "Rolla Rama" was pretty much the only real entertainment left. So, you can imagine the love I had for roller skating.

I remember skating for hours, losing at "Limbo" or happily falling on my ass countless times while attempting to skate backward or "Shoot the Duck". I learned all of those white trash trends from my parents. They had both worked at the Rolla Rama when they were in their teens and could effortlessly skate backward. A skill I still haven't been able to master. I think everyone who lived in my town worked at the Rolla Rama at one point. It was like a rite of passage.

Jobs in my minuscule hometown were limited. As a teen, you either roller-skated or life-guarded. Then, once you got old enough to join the workforce officially, your choices were between three factories. You could either make washers and dryers, popcorn, or clock in over on the east side of town at the Marion Power Shovel. I still have no clue what they do there. I assume some sort of futuristic, electric-powered shovels are involved, though.

My mother went above and beyond for my birthday parties. I was an only child — and not only that, I was a miracle baby. My mother was told she would never have children. Not by my father or by the government. No, a doctor told her this. So, I was spoiled. Very, very spoiled.

My mother would order endless pizzas, prepare multiple homemade cookie trays, and buy so much soda pop you could swim in it. So many balloons would be bunched up and tied to the old corner booth tables they would float a few inches above the dirty checkered linoleum floors.

One last item that I could always count on having

on my birthday was a custom made cake.

Every year, my mom had a themed birthday cake made for me. The cake themes were based primarily on current events in my life. My mom had her own language — a "Cake Code", if you will.

When I moved from Indiana to Los Angeles, my mother had a cake made that featured me, my fiancée, at the time, and our dog Fraiser surfing on a big tidal wave. "Have fun in California!" It read in delicious bright yellow lettering.

When I got cast in my first film, Chopping Block, my mother turned the movie poster into a sheet cake. "Congratulations" was written in blood red to honor the quirky horror film.

When I turned thirty, she gave me a cake with the Man of Steel himself proudly displayed in riveting multiple colors and sky sprinkles. Because her little man was turning into a yup, "Superman".

Though she spoke in "Cake Code", the language itself felt familiar. That's because that language was Love. My mother loved me. I loved her, too.

I haven't had one of my mother's custom made cakes in almost five years now. However, I do have a voicemail of my mother singing "Happy Birthday" to me one last time. I think that's better than a cake. A lot fewer calories, at least.

When someone passes on, we are the ones who are left to decide how we will carry that person with us. I've been thinking about that a lot lately. The weight of loss. How do you let go of someone without forgetting them? How do you carry someone with you without allowing the extra weight to hold you back?

Just like you do everything else: Little by little. Day by day.

Each day, I let go of a little more anger, loneliness, and fear. I let go of the heavy stuff, and I keep what's important. Her voice, her memory, and her aspirations for me. I celebrate with her. I cry with her. We still talk quite often.

Like learning the proper ways to exercise at the

gym, I've learned how to carry the weight of loss with me so that it makes me stronger.

I'm writing this story on the eve of my 37th birthday. I can't sleep. It's past 2 A.M., and I'm wide awake and thinking about my mother and her wonderfully cheesy, personalized birthday cakes. It's one of her many characteristic traditions that I miss the most.

I don't have any plans to celebrate yet, but I think I'll go roller skating.

IT GETS BETTER.
IT GETS BETTER.
IT GETS BETTER.
IT GETS BETTER.
IT GETS BETTER.
IT GETS BETTER.
IT GETS BETTER.

NEPHEW: WHY DO YOU ALWAYS WATCH SAD TV SHOWS?

ME: BECAUSE LIFE IS SAD. NOW GO TO BED.

NEPHEW: IT'S ONLY 6PM.

ME: FINE. I'LL GO TO BED.

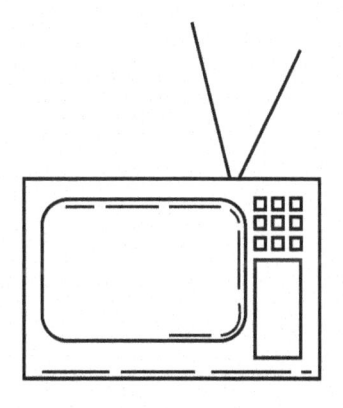

I DID ONE OF THOSE 23 AND ME TESTS.

TURNS OUT I'M 100% DREAMBOAT.

THE FRESH PRINCE OF BEL-AIR MUST HAVE BEEN THE MOST ANNOYING DUDE TO GO ON A FIRST DATE WITH.

HER: SO, TELL ME ABOUT YOURSELF.

FRESH PRINCE: WWWEEELLLL, THIS IS A STORY ALL ABOUT HOW MY LIFE GOT FLIPPED-TURNED UPSIDE DOWN...

KILL YOUR SELFIE.

11/09/18

<u>**KILL YOUR SELFIE.**</u>
Work on becoming the image that you are portraying yourself to be online.

<u>**KILL YOUR SELFIE.**</u>
Stop trying to live up to other people's images on their social media. That is not who they are. Just as you are not who you are pretending to be.

<u>**KILL YOUR SELFIE.**</u>
The only thing you can do is focus on becoming a better version of yourself.

LOVE IS NOT DISCOVERED IN
THE THROES OF PASSION.

IT'S HIDING IN THE QUIET
NIGHTS SPENT ON THE COUCH.

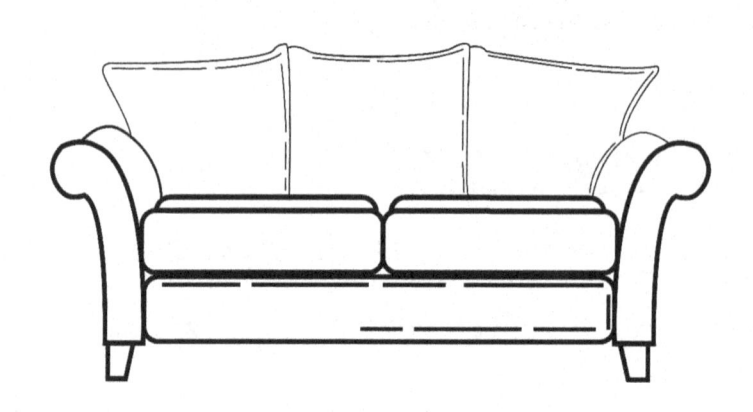

THEY BURIED MY STEPFATHER IN THE WRONG CEMETERY PLOT.

Wayne died in the winter when the air was brisk, the ground was blanketed in snow, and our hearts were frozen and fragile.

Once spring came, I received a phone call from my mother. She was hysterical — an absolute wreck. She stopped crying just long enough to tell me about the situation. It sucked, but the only resolution was to dig his coffin back up and move Wayne over to the correct plot.

I tried to cheer my mother up and said, "Look at the bright side, Ma, we get to see Wayne again!" My mother gasped, then there was a brief pause before a giant laugh flooded the phone.

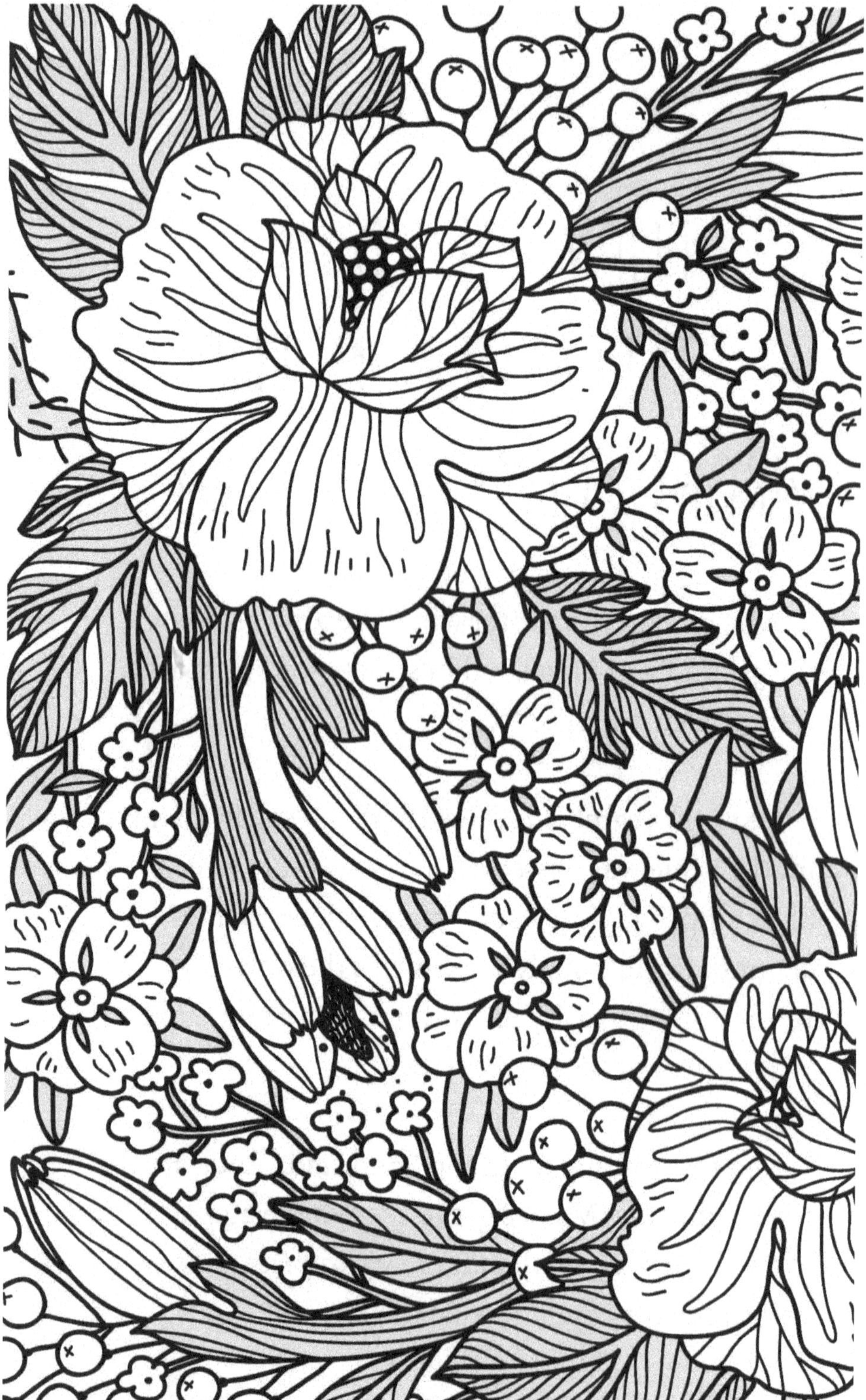

YOU HAVE TO LET THEM GO SO YOU CAN GROW.

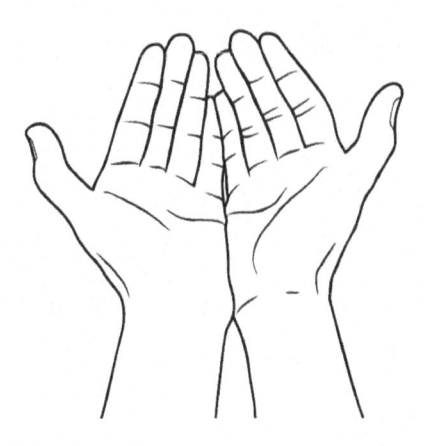

The friends and family who are not supporting you while you work on yourself, or who value their hurt over your mental health are not the people you need in your life.

We have all made a stand or set a boundary where a friend or family member responded with disappointment or shame. Fuck those people. Those are not the people you need in your life. Let them go. Clear some space for new people.

This happens a lot of times when people try and get sober. Some friends only want to party, and when you try and better yourself and stop partying, they have trouble supporting you. They selfishly value their own needs over yours and will ridicule or sometimes dismiss you from their lives. Good. Let them go.

You need room to grow, so don't be afraid to let go and get rid of those toxic relationships. You can't grow flowers in a pile of rocks, and that's who those people are. Stubborn, unmovable stones that are weighing you down.

THERAPIST: HOW HAVE YOU BEEN SLEEPING?

ME: I SLEEP GREAT! I'VE BEEN GETTING AROUND 3-4 HOURS A NIGHT.

THERAPIST: WELL, THA--

ME: THEN ANOTHER 10-12 HOURS AFTER I GIVE UP ON LIFE AFTER LUNCH.

MEDIUM SIZE TALK

I like to wear headphones or AirPods whenever I'm out in public. I enjoy being unavailable, as I'm not great at casual conversation. I'm not shy; I just don't care about what a lot of other people care about. Don't get me wrong: I care about many common ground issues like shutting down the zoos, stopping sex traffickers, and all that fun stuff. However, I do not keep up with the Kardashians or the Dallas Cowboys.

I never know the score. I have no clue who won the latest season of "The Voice," and I would rather pour hot coffee inside my urethra than

talk about how "it might rain this Thursday".
I thought wearing headphones while I was out in public was a pretty good sign that I wasn't interested in having a conversation. I was wrong. With a low, monotone mumbling, my Uber driver's voice cut through my Counting Crows playlist.

I removed one of my AirPods like we all do when interacting with strangers, as if to say, "You are not worthy of both of my ears. You may have only half my attention."

My best friend is always badgering me about talking to strangers more often. He claims I'm missing out on the "true essence of life". I told him I wasn't any good at it. He argued that I had built my entire life literally on the task of talking to strangers.

However, being a comedian is different. When I'm performing on stage, I have no problem engaging with people. There are lights, microphones, pressure, and adrenaline.

Maybe that's the answer: I need to start carrying

a miniature spotlight with me at all times. That way, when forced to interact with someone in public, I'll just plug in the spotlight, and it's showtime, baby! Strangers instantly become hecklers, and I always know what to say to them.

It's different from being out in the wild. When I'm out in the world, I like to play the role of a humble observer. When I'm tooling around the city, I try very hard to disrupt very little.

Here and there, I will capture a funny voice or phrase. If something makes me laugh hard or if I find myself mocking someone's tone, I'll make a note of it.

For example, at a dive bar in Cleveland, I once overheard a man tell his friend, "All moms are hot now." I laughed at first, but then, later that night, I found myself thinking about it. "He's right. All moms are hot now."

They all wear yoga pants, hike, and drink soy milk. My mother never drank soy milk.

One afternoon, when I was on tour in

Indianapolis, I was on an elevator questioning my life choices, as you do in an elevator. Was I missing out on "the essence of life," as my friend had suggested?

The elevator doors opened, and a middle-aged woman in sloppy cargo shorts and a faded, dark brown tank top walked on. A floor later, an older African American gentleman in a freshly ironed black suit boarded the small elevator.

Feeling brave, I attempted to make small talk with the well-dressed man.

"That's a great suit. You look sharp, dude," I nervously blurted out.

"Oh, well, thank you," he said. "I'm going to a funeral."

"Well, have fun!" I shot back at the stranger, a broad smile on my face.

The woman in cargo shorts slowly turned her head and stared at me in shock. I couldn't figure out why, so I frantically thought back on what I had just said.

"Fuck. Fuck. Fuck. What did I say?! Nice suit ... You look sharp ... Have fun ... Fuck. What am I missing?" I anxiously scrolled our brief conversation in my mind.

FUNERAL! The man said he was going to a funeral, and I said, "Have fun."

"I'm sorry, I thought you said you were going to a wedding, not a funeral," I said, desperately trying to cover my mistake.

"Oh ... no, no. A funeral," the well-dressed man somberly repeated.

"Same difference, am I right?" I said jokingly, in an attempt to break up the awkwardness.

Once again, the woman's head slowly turned toward me in disappointment. A few moments later, the elevator doors opened. I haven't made small talk since. That was three years ago.

"Where ya headed?" My Uber driver shouted.

She knew where. She was driving us there, for fuck's sake. Plus, she didn't need me to tell her where we were going. Her wristwatch could give her better turn-by-turn directions than any human born after 1985 ever could.

She didn't need directions. She needed attention. She had a large frame and a warmth that I felt in the backseat. She seemed lively and spoke with confidence. I hate people like this. Happy. You know the type. The kind of person who gets a flat tire and says something stupid like, "Thank God I blew that tire. I meant to buy new tires. Must have been a blessing in disguise."

I blew a tire once. I was driving to a gig in Arizona, and the temperature was a ripe 112 degrees. It was far from a blessing in disguise.

"Ohio," I answered. "Going home to see my family," I continued, like a fucking idiot.

I didn't know why I was volunteering information like that last part. That is what one might refer to as "small talk," and the only thing I hate more than happy people is, you guessed it, small talk.

Small talk is so uneventful, but you can't walk up to a stranger on the street and say, "Space, am I right? What the fuck is going on up there? Let's talk about it!" No, we are taught to be polite and say things like, "Nice day, isn't it?"

I'd rather be gagged with a pre-teen's dirty sock than engage in anything less than medium-sized talk.

"That sounds nice," she shot back at me.
Of course, she thought so. It was all part of her forced customer service.

"I'm not from here, either," she said. "I live out by Santa Monica now, and I don't miss my hometown at all. I can tell you that much. What's it like living here in Hollywood?" She inquired.

I hate when people say "Hollywood" instead of "Los Angeles". I mean, I know they are different things and that people are using "Hollywood" correctly, but it just feels dirty. It feels like they're showing off. It's like when a security guard flashes their badge. Yes, technically, that is a badge, but we all know you're just a janitor with a cleaner uniform.

That's what we all are here in Hollywood: janitors.

We are all janitors who are pretending to be more important than we are. The little blue checkmarks at the end of our names on social media are our badges, and we can't wait to flash them to strangers.

"It's ... uh, okay, I guess," I responded, still holding the AirPod a few inches from my left ear.

"Oh, that's what's up," she said while making an illegal right turn on red. "I'm surprised your family isn't coming out here. My friends and family are always bugging me to come out and visit. They think I'm living the dream out here in Hollywood. When's the last time your family came out here to visit you?" She asked.

I felt embarrassed that I had to think about the answer. After a long pause, I responded with a stunted response. "Umm ... I don't - Uh, I don't think any of my family have been out here. Yeah ... None of them have ever come to visit me here," I stammered.

The answer cut me in half.

I had never given it any thought. I'm always the one traveling, so it's not like I don't ever see my family. I do. I make the time to see them when I'm touring in nearby towns, but not one of them has stepped one foot inside my world here in "Hollywood".

Wow.

I was split in two. I felt like I was bleeding out in the back of a poor man's taxi service. All my secrets slowly oozed out of me, one by one.

The driver didn't know how to react, either. I could feel it. Her next question staggered out of her mouth so poorly; it could have been my father leaving a small-town pub late on a Saturday night.

"How, uh - How long have you lived out here?" Each word could barely stand on its own.

"Seven years," I said with a newly acquired sadness.

There was another long pause, and then the stranger spoke again.

"Oh, man. That fucking sucks," she said in a comforting manner.

Another tense pause floated in the air before I popped it like one of those giant gender-reveal balloons.

"Well, to be fair, most of my family is dead. So I can't blame them for not coming to see me." I said with a large grin.

I was hoping she would appreciate my dark sense of humor and that her laughter would cut through the awkwardness and the pain. I wanted to go back to listening to "Rain King" with both of my ears.

It didn't.

It didn't because there was no laughter. Only silence. A silence that would last the rest of the car ride.

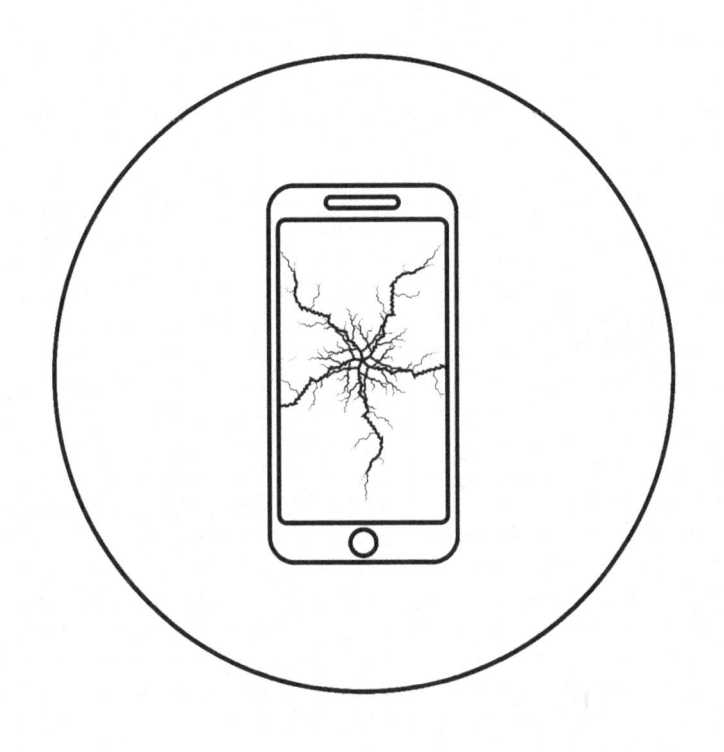

RIDE OVERSHARE

HECKLER: I HAVE FIVE KIDS.

ME: NO WAY! HOW OLD IS YOUR YOUNGEST?

HECKLER: SHE'S TWO YEARS OLD AND SHE IS AUTISTIC. SO YEAH, TRY AND BE FUNNY NOW.

ME: SIR... THERE IS NO WAY SOMEBODY FUCKED YOU TWO YEARS AGO.

7/04/18

There is no lifeguard on duty. No one is coming to save you. You are going to have to learn how to fucking swim.

AN OCTOPUS HAS THREE
HEARTS. TWO OF THEM ARE
USED TO PUMP BLOOD TO ITS
GILLS, THE THIRD ONE THEY
WEAR ON THEIR SLEEVE.

INVEST IN THINGS THAT ARE BIGGER THAN YOU.

FOREVER JUNE

My head laid in my mother's lap as she slowly stroked her fingers through my hair. It was my favorite thing my mother would do. Sure, home cooking was nice, but this always made me feel like a child again.

It was my mother's 66th birthday and we sat out on her old wooden porch swing. Rocking back and forth as a cool June breeze gently blew through the weathered cracks of the back deck of her cozy Ohio home.

Neither of us knew this would be the last time we would sit in that old porch swing together.

My mother's hanging chimes danced gracefully in the wind. They collided together in a way that all chimes to do that produce beautiful yet slightly annoying music that still haunts me to this day.

She confessed that she finally sold my cemetery plot. Yes, my mother had already picked out and paid for my grave. I hated that. It felt like I would eventually be moving back in with my mother after I died. So I asked her to sell it.

Maybe that's what purgatory is. You end up living in your dead parent's basement in the afterlife. Nevermind that sounds like Hell. Not purgatory.

I told my mother I wanted to be cremated because I believe we will all be living in some form of artificial intelligence simulation soon anyway, so go ahead and burn my body. I won't need it once we all live in the cloud. I don't mean Heaven; I mean, Dropbox — that kind of cloud.

She asked me if I planned on keeping the house and moving back to town when she was dead and gone. I laughed; she didn't. However, when she died just a few days later, I did have a conversation with my now ex-fiancé about doing just that. I suggested that we move back to Ohio for a year or so. That way I could clean out the house and grieve at a comfortable pace.

But we didn't do anything sensible like that.

No, instead, I went back on tour just ten short days after my mother died. My fiancé and I ended up taking turns flying back and forth from Los Angeles to clean out my mother's house.

We emptied my childhood home in thirty days flat. Impressive? Sure. Recommend it? Abso-fucking-lutley not. Mentally, I was a mess but hey, the house was empty and on the market.

One night before my late show in Portland, I took a phone call from my fiancé and her father. They told me they were almost finished with my mother's bedroom but weren't sure what to do with her large king-sized bed. I had forgotten about how narrow the hallways were in my mother's old mid-size country home.

When we moved in, my mother had her second-story window taken out so that my father and a few neighbors could pull that king-sized mattress up with a rope. It was a hillbilly crane system. All you needed was some bungee cords from the Dollar Store and a few Miller Lites and brother, you're in business.

After my show in Portland was over, I listened on speakerphone as my fiancé's father cut my mother's mattress into pieces with an electric saw he found in my dead step-father's garage. It was the first time that saw had been used since Wayne, my step-father, passed a year prior.

I never got to properly say goodbye to that house, my mother's belongings, or even her. All I am left with are memories of that cool June breeze and those hanging chimes dancing in the wind.

I spoke to my mother the day before she died. Her voice was cold, reserved almost, and a thousand miles away. Neither of us knew that that would be the last time we would speak.

Even if we had known, what would I have said? I love you? She knew that I loved her. She knew that I would miss her deeply as well.

What do you say to someone before they die other than, "Please don't fucking die!"

Looking back on that phone call, I wish I would have said thank you. I wish I could thank my mother for being such a strong role model. A beacon of light and joy. Someone that I could aspire to be like when I grow up. I wish I could have thanked her for all of her hard work and sacrifice. I wish I would have said a lot of things, but I blew our conversation off like we all do when our moms call us.

It physically pains me that I can't remember our last conversation. The shame weighs on me not only in my mind but in my heart and my fucking gut. Eating away at me as if I ingested battery acid.

It's not my fault. I don't remember our last conversation because it was about nothing. More than likely, we chatted about the weather or something funny the dog did. The irony; Everyday life stuff, on the eve of my mother's death.

The night she passed, I was performing at a brewery about five hours north of Los Angeles. I had driven up there in a van with five other comedians.

They all went out drinking after our show with some of the audience members, but I retreated to the hotel and passed out early. I was exhausted from the drive up that morning. Plus, I was the only sober one in the group. I was also engaged at the time. So the task of drinking with a group of strange women in a small town didn't excite me.

A few hours after the other comics returned to our hotel, I woke up to a phone call from my fiancé. I heard her holding back tears as she took a deep breath. Then she told me that my mother had died peacefully in her sleep. A phone call that I'm sure still haunts her, just as much as it haunts me.

I hung up the phone and woke up my very drunk friends around four o'clock in the morning. They had just fallen alseep about an hour before this. We all loaded up in the same van we had just gotten out of a few hours earlier and began our journey back to Los Angeles.

If I could make a recommendation here, it would be to hire a group of comedians to hang out with you after someone you love passes away. There was no uncomfortable silence for the entire five-hour ride home. No, instead the air was filled with unfiltered and dark-humored jokes about my recently deceased mother and I wouldn't have wanted it any other way.

I was raised to laugh in the face of tragedy. My family always dealt with hard topics with even harder laughter. My mother and grandmother were two of the strongest and most stubborn women I have ever met. They refused to let life get the best of them.

I was raised to laugh instead of cry. To find something odd, or peculiar while sifting through the aftermath and shine the biggest spotlight on it until all that was left was just that; light.

Every comedian that I dropped off that morning ended with a long embrace, a few tears, and a joke that would make the devil himself blush.

A few days later, I found myself back in Ohio. I sat on my mother's old wooden porch swing and began to rock back and forth as the cool June breeze blew through my hair like my mother's fingers did just a few days before.

Even though she wasn't sitting next to me, I still talked to her about boring everyday life stuff like the weather and something funny the dog did as her hanging chimes danced gracefully in the wind.

JUNE GLOOM

I PASSED A BILLBOARD THAT READ, "LET GOD FIX IT."

MY FIRST THOUGHT WAS, "WHAT IF IT'S A PLUMBING ISSUE?"

3/22/17

Death makes us wish for second chances, but we know that's impossible. Instead, death should motivate us to be the best version of ourselves the first time around.

TAUROPHOBIA IS A FEAR OF BULLS.

TAROTPHOBIA IS A FEAR OF PEOPLE WHO READ TAROT CARDS.

I WAS IN SIOUX FALLS SOUTH DAKOTA RECENTLY. SUCH A SMALL TOWN. SO SMALL I WAS SCARED TO OPEN ANY OF MY DATING APPS. WHEN I FINALLY DID, MY FRONT FACING CAMERA CAME ON AND THE APP SAID, "YOU'RE BETTER OFF JUST FUCKING YOURSELF THIS WEEKEND."

NEVER MAKE PERMANENT DECISIONS THAT ARE BASED ON TEMPORARY FEELINGS.

IT RAINED FOR SEVEN DAYS STRAIGHT AFTER MY MOTHER DIED.

The first morning it didn't; we had her funeral. As soon as the preacher laid the final flower on top of my mother's casket, storm clouds began to roll in.

I want to believe it was my mother who kept us dry that morning. You know, so we didn't mess up our hair.

Hair was always very important to my mother.

SORRY, I'VE BEEN REALLY SAD SINCE WE LOST GRANDPA.

DO YOU REMEMBER THE LAST PLACE YOU HAD HIM? MAYBE TRY CHECKING THE PANTS YOU WERE WEARING THAT DAY...

STOP TRYING TO FIND "THE ONE" AND WORK ON BECOMING "THE ONE" FOR SOMEONE ELSE.

When a relationship goes sour, there are a lot of roadblocks before the breakup. You find yourself doubting that someone else exists in the world that could love you the way the person you are currently with loves you.

Ask yourself this; If the person you are currently with loved you the way you wanted to be loved, then why would you be looking to escape the relationship?

I'm sure there are reasons you are thinking about staying with this person, just like there are reasons you want to leave. The best thing to do is to ask yourself these two things; "What are they bringing to the table?," and also, "what am I bringing to the table?"

You want to be with someone that is bringing comparable items to the relationship. Balance is what keeps a relationship stable. It's simply not fair for one person to be stuck carrying the weight for both of you.

Think of it as hiking. Would you find it enjoyable to carry both backpacks? Of course not, you'd never make it. You would end up setting up camp and getting comfortable. That's what being in an unhealthy relationship is.

You've set up camp, but a tent out in the mountains is not an ideal place to make a permanent home.

It is crucial that you are brutally honest with yourself, as well. Your life is not only at stake, but so is your happiness.

Most of the time, the hardest decision to make is usually the right one.

You need to ask yourself if you are truly happy in your current relationship, and if not, what would it take for you to be? If you are confident that your partner is willing and able to put in the work, well, then, by all means, do it. But do not stay with someone who isn't. You have wasted enough time with them, and there are plenty of other people out there that are waiting for you and what you bring to the table.

MY HAUNTED HOLIDAYS

My mother loved Christmas. Around the Holidays, every square inch of our two-story, middle-class, Midwestern home would be covered in decor. Our back porch door even had a plastic animated Santa Claus face that would spring alive when anyone would come within two hundred feet of our home. It would let out a bellowing laugh and sing in the middle of the night.

This haunted Santa wouldn't wait for company to stop by. No, sometimes a strong wind would find its way to our doorstep, and that jolly old Saint Nick would greet that gust of wind with giant laughs and a three-minute version of Jingle Bells, complete with orchestra music in the background. I don't know where my mother found such a torturous device, but we owned two of them.

One of them mysteriously broke one year. Yet, we still hung its lifeless head on our back door like some sick tribal warning.

My mother would have a manger scene displayed in every room of our vast country home — some with fictional characters. Like the one that sat on top of the cabinet in the bathroom, it featured the Mickey Mouse gang admiring baby Jesus. How festive.

The most beautiful set was displayed on top of the microwave in the kitchen with pride. It had everything: fake snow flooring, fencing, and even some livestock. One year, we were a Wiseman short, so I replaced him with a spare Ninja Turtle action figure. I liked adding the idea of Michelangelo bringing nun chucks and pizza to the unauthorized story of baby Jesus, but my mother failed to see the humor.

We had a fake tree that we stored up in the loft of our garage. The same loft I used to retreat to when I was a teenager and smoke cigarettes and look at deteriorating Playboy magazines. Like most Playboy magazines that teenage boys owned, most of the pages stuck together. Not for the reasons you think, no, it was because I kept them stored in the damp loft space above our riding lawnmower.

Because of my deviant stash of damp loft paraphernalia that I was hiding, I always would be the one who crawled up and dragged down the boxed-up tree every year. I would pull the large cardboard box behind me along the first snowfall and the rough gravel of our driveway. Then Mom and I would unpack the branches piece by piece and lay them out neatly onto the living room floor before assembling the old family fire hazard.

The Christmas ballads of Mariah Carey and Bing Crosby would fill our home with a familiar warmth as they blared from my step-father's six-disc CD changer. Strands of what seemed like never-ending multi-colored lights would be pouring out of large Rubbermaid totes, each neatly labeled on the side in perfect cursive, "Nancy's Christmas Stuff" as if Santa himself wrote it.

Hours we would spend decorating the tree, which, in my opinion, was way too fucking big for our middle-class living room. It was tall and round and had big chunks missing around the belly that my mother always fluffed out and was able to cover up.

I never had the patience for such a task. I would tug and pull and fluff on a branch for about ten seconds, which in teenager time felt like ages. Then I'd angrily give up and move on to the next bare branch. But not my mother. She would take the time to do it right. My mother was a master of this craft. She knew how to manipulate every individual hair on those branches into looking like they were full of life and could hold the weight of ten thousand pounds of Christmas joy.

The star on top of our tall old tree used to belong to her grandmother. It would barely graze the rough spackling of our ceiling as the sides of the tree would spill over onto the top of the arms and backs of my mother's white on white couch and loveseat.

Christmas was a special time for my mother, but I never got around to asking why it meant so much to her. Questions like that, you don't think about when you're a kid. When you're young, most of the questions you have revolve around food and what time you get to eat said food.

I hated Christmas for the first few years after my mother died. I didn't want to celebrate it ever again. I yearned to be one of those people who would escape to Hawaii for a long holiday. I thought I would be happy becoming that dickhead who sends a Christmas card from the beach with a clever pun like, "Wish You Were Beer". I'd be wearing bright floral swim trunks while holding a Bud Light high above my head like a trophy. But that's not who I am or who I want to be.

I still have a few boxes stored in the small town where I grew up, labeled, "Nancy's Christmas Stuff". I don't know what's in them or if I'll ever be strong enough to open them without her.

Nancy's
Christmas
Stuff

I NEED TO QUIT SPRAY PAINTING "IN THE NAME OF LOVE" ON STOP SIGNS.

DO NOT LET THE FEAR OF "WHAT IF" STOP YOU FROM ANSWERING THE QUESTION OF "WHAT NOW?"

Take action today. Use that fear to motivate you. Take action now. Don't let "What If" stop you from taking action on "What Now".

CHANGE IS NOT EASY, BUT IT IS ESSENTIAL FOR GROWTH.

DOG: SAY IT.

ME: NO.

DOG: COME ON... SAAAYYY IT...

ME: UGH, FINE.

DOG: WHAT IS THE NUMBER ONE SEXUAL POSITION FEMALES LIKE?

ME: DOGGY STY--

DOG: YES!! DOGGY STYLE!! THAT'S RIGHT, BABY! DON'T FORGET IT!

THIS IS YOUR BRAIN ON HUGS.

ONE LAST PINTEREST PROJECT

I was getting interviewed on a podcast about self-help recently, and the host asked me what advice I would give to someone before they committed suicide. Before he could finish the question, I blurted out, "Don't do it."

"Then I would follow it up with telling them that it gets better. Even if it doesn't feel like it now, or ever has. Even if your life is worse than it's ever been, it gets better." I continued.

On a long car ride back to Los Angeles from Phoenix after a weekend of shows, I confessed to my friend, Ken, that I thought that my story ends in suicide.

Not now or anytime soon, I reassured him. I don't have a plan or even really thought about how I would do it. But yeah, eventually, I think that's how my story ends. I don't want to get old.

Nothing about getting old looks fun. Not even the sweet parking spots are worth it.

At the time, I didn't have anyone depending on me. So why would I wait around and die from a heart attack on some toilet in Oklahoma when I could do it myself? I've always been into DIY projects, and suicide seems like the ultimate last Pinterest project to mark off my list.

My friend was mortified and taken back by how casual I was talking about it.

I didn't understand his shock. I thought everybody thought about it. I thought everybody viewed suicide as an option.

"What? You've never thought about killing yourself?" I asked.

"Never." He said confidently.

Ken went on to share an idea with me, something I will shamefully admit I had never considered before this conversation.

Gratitude.

He talked about being grateful in life. How lucky we are to experience it. How he makes a list of things that he is thankful for in his life almost weekly. How wonderful getting old is going to be, even if I don't have anyone depending on me, he urged me to stay alive to see where humanity itself ends up going. He was like if one of those 'Hang in There' posters came to life.

Gratitude. Wow. Such a strange new concept.
"Is this is a religious thing?" I said half-kidding.
"No - Come on, fuck off. It's something that I do that helps me when life sucks. It's something I have practiced a lot while getting sober. It helps me remember why I'm sober and how important life is." He shared.

"It doesn't have to be anything big either. I wrote down naps the other day." He continued.

"Naps?" I questioned.

"Yeah. I feel grateful that I have a job that allows me to take a nap in the middle of the day. See, so like nothing big. Sure, I'm thankful for other shit like being able to walk, and good health but naps, bro. The little things in life that you might be overlooking." He explained with a grin.

It sounded almost too good to be true. Everything always does, I'm a glass half empty kind of guy by default.

I'm not even that negative. I'm more worried than anything else. I don't think the glass is half empty. I think, "it's too close to the edge, and the dog is going to knock it off the table, and we are going to have take the dog to the vet to get the glass out of his paws," kind of guy.

"If my grandma wasn't alive, I would have killed myself after my mother died. But I couldn't do that to her. It wouldn't have been fair. I couldn't add more loss to her life." I admitted to Ken.

"Well, I'm glad you didn't." Ken declared.

I'm glad I didn't kill myself either because I can see now that it gets better. I am so happy these days. I am happier than I ever have been in my entire life. I am on the other side of things, and I have a message I want to share with everyone who felt how I felt; Alone. Unheard. Lonely. Depressed. Unloved. Overlooked. Left behind...

This message is for you; It gets better. Keep swimming.

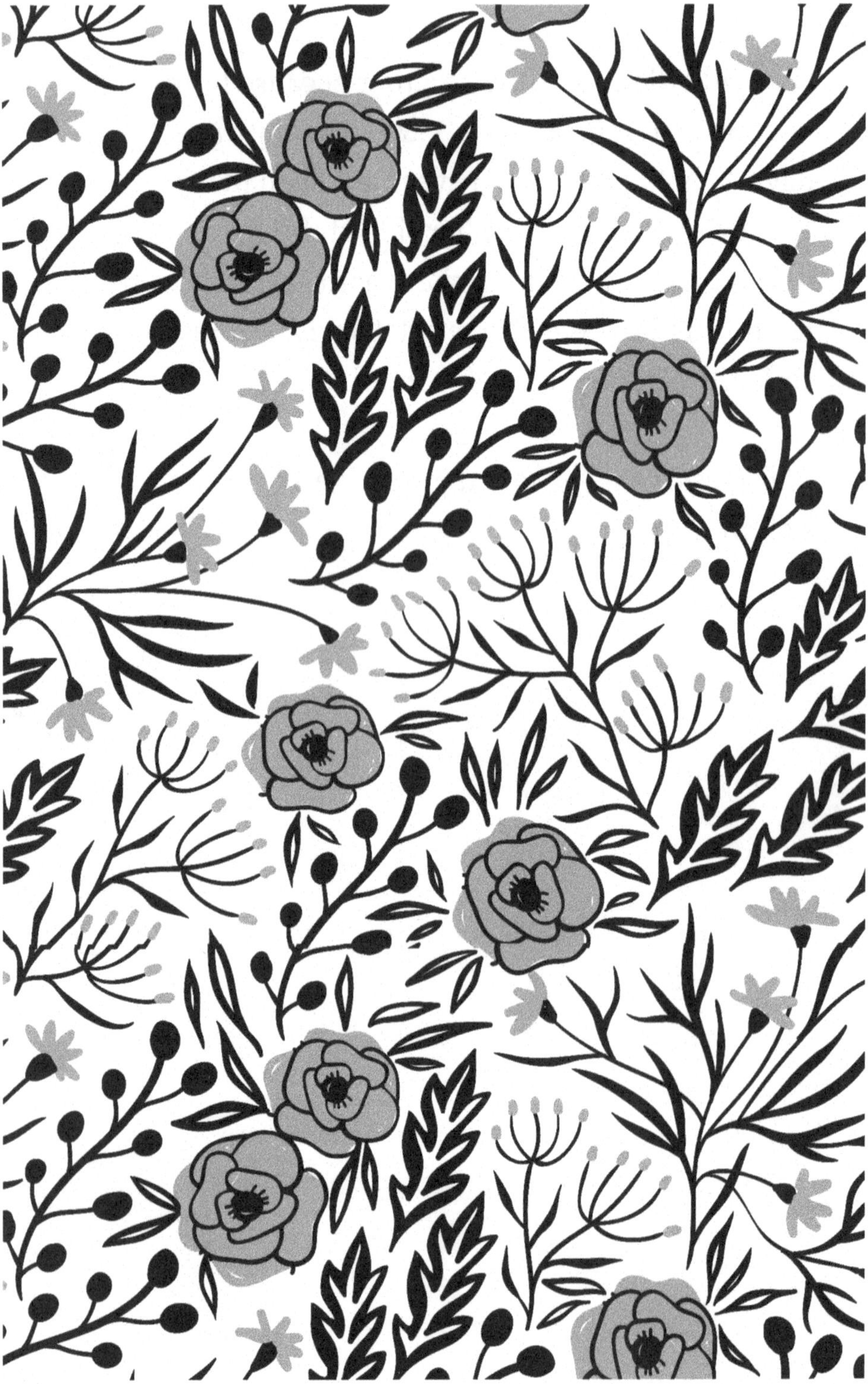

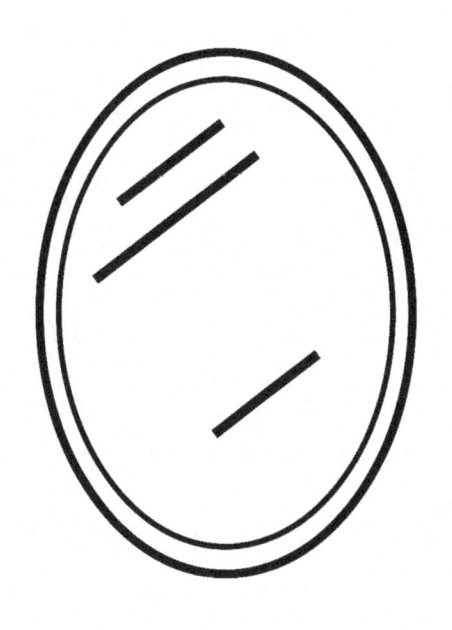

I'VE GOTTEN INTO AN ODD HABIT OF GAZING INTO THE BATHROOM MIRROR AND ASKING MYSELF, "WHAT ARE YOU DOING WITH YOUR LIFE?" THEN AGGRESSIVELY RESPONDING, "WHATEVER THE FUCK I WANT!!"

I THINK THIS IS THE LAST PHASE BEFORE I JOIN FIGHT CLUB.

I JUST SIGNED UP FOR "CHICKEN TINDER." IT'S GREAT! THEY SHOW ME PHOTOS OF CHICKEN TENDERS FROM RESTAURANTS IN MY AREA AND IF I LIKE THEM WE MEET UP.

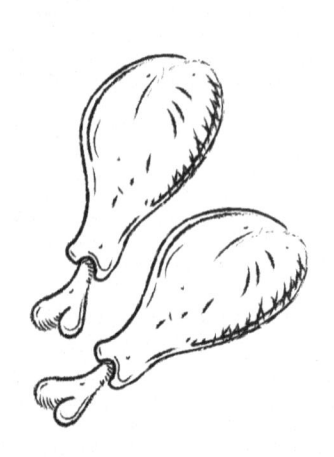

IF YOU ARE NOT HAPPY WITH YOUR LIFE, YOUR JOB, OR YOUR RELATIONSHIP, ONLY YOU HAVE THE POWER TO REWRITE YOUR STORY. ONLY YOU CONTROL YOUR NARRATIVE.

I am no better than you. I am not any further along than you. I don't have any more answers than you. But I do know this; we are the stories we tell ourselves. So stop telling yourself the story you don't want to hear.

You are the only one saying those shitty things. I guarantee that the people who are close to you are asking, "Why don't they change? They are so unhappy, why don't they do something about it?"

I can prove those close friends notice because the minute you do finally change and switch things up those same friends are going to come around and say, "I always thought that you should have blah blah blah..."

Everybody is waiting for you. You're late. It's your fucking party, and you're late.

THE ONLY MAMMALS THAT
EXPERIENCE MENOPAUSE ARE
ELEPHANTS, HUMPBACK WHALES
AND YOUR FAT MOM.

6/08/18

Sometimes in life, we fall down. When that happens, people encourage you with generic phrases like, "Get right back up!" - "Don't let life keep you down!" I think they're wrong. I think sometimes you have to lay in your mess. You need to look at the damage. I think we, as a society, shouldn't judge people on how fast they get back on their feet but instead on who they become after they have the strength to stand.

Falling down fucking sucks. Lay in your mess and learn from it.

LUKE WARM WATER

"I'm leaving for the day," Robert shouted into the depths of a big hollowed-out tree.

Robert and his wife, Vanessa, were doing very well for themselves. These were hard times for squirrels. Some squirrels were sharing a tree with two to three other families. But not Robert and Vanessa. No, it was just the two of them in a big redwood near a large park. That's right; they were doing so well; they were living parkside.

"Don't forget to pick up an extra acorn! Donny and Faye are coming for dinner!" Vanessa shouted back. And with that, Robert was off to work.

Vanessa's heart always sank a little after she heard her husband scurry down the giant redwood. She no longer had a job, and their babies were full-grown and long gone. The ones she kept and didn't eat, that is. So, most afternoons, Vanessa would be left to entertain herself. She never got into any trouble. No, she mostly would learn new recipes or tidy up. She was famous in their small community for making the best banana nut bread this side of the pond. Her secret, well, were the fresh nuts she and Robert would bring home from their evening walks, of course. Those and a few chocolate chips that is.

The old tree, although large and spacious, was also quite drafty. Leaves and bugs would find their way inside, so Vanessa spent most afternoons chasing them both out onto the ground below. Neither of which gave her much trouble.

However, isolation was not Vanessa's friend. No, lately, Vanessa had felt as if the hole she and Robert had scurried themselves into years ago had begun to close up. She had mentioned this to Robert, but he blamed it on the weather changing and went back to reading his Sunday morning newspaper.

Vanessa didn't know what she was feeling exactly, but she knew it had to do with much more than just the seasons changing. She not only felt different, but she began behaving oddly as well.

Vanessa had begun a new habit of crawling back into bed after her husband left for work. Sure, she could be hiding a lot worse things from her husband than sleep, but for some reason, she didn't feel like she could tell Robert. He worked so hard, and he did so much for their family. He would surely judge her. Maybe even leave her for a younger, more active squirrel.

But that wasn't all that she was hiding.

Some mornings she would have ice cream for breakfast. Some mornings she wouldn't eat at all. Some mornings she would get up early and go for a run but then crawl back into bed until dinner time. Some mornings she would fake like she was sick to get out of visiting with friends or family. She would blame things like the lack of sleep or the weather, as Robert suggested, but secretly, she felt fine and was well-rested. Hell, all she did was rest.

Robert was a good husband. He never questioned her. He would just kiss her on her forehead and tell her to feel better before trudging out to take on their social chores.

She didn't want to lose that. She didn't want to lose him. She knew she was selfish, but she had made peace with that.

One afternoon, she thought, "What would I do without Robert?" Then a more dangerous idea came about, "What would Robert do without me?"

She stood naked in front of the mirror a few days later, examining the areas she was unhappy with and ignoring the ones she liked. "Who would want this? Who would find this attractive?" She grumbled aloud to herself as she grabbed a handful of fat and fur.

"If I could just lose three ounces, then I'd be happy," she convinced herself.

She started a diet that week, and in six weeks, she did it. She lost those three ounces. She was strutting around the old redwood home with her tail trimmed and her hair done like Robert liked. Vanessa had a slight curl in the front. Robert loved that curl. Rumor had it, Vanessa had a hint of skunk in her family, so sometimes the hair on her head would have a tiny curl to it when it got wet. When she was younger, it would drive all the male squirrels crazy. It kept Robert on his toes, that's for sure. Truth be told, that tiny curl is probably a big part of why Robert asked her to marry him so early on in their lives.

On average, squirrels live to be around seven years old. There is some folklore about a squirrel in Michigan near the Great Lakes, who lived to be eleven, but nobody could ever confirm it. Most everyone believes that he had been stuffed, and some squirrels saw him on a shelf in a bar and had mistaken him as being alive.

Still, seven years was the average, and Robert and Vanessa have been married for almost four years. That's over half of their lives.

Vanessa paraded around the redwood for a couple of weeks in her new trim frame, but then the sadness kicked in again. She didn't know if it was the isolation or what, but she found herself in front of the mirror once more. This time, the problem area was that tiny curl in her hair. She had begun to hate it. She felt like the very thing that made her stand out was the same thing that defined her, and she did not want to be defined by a tiny string of curly hair. No, she had a lot more to offer the world than that.

So one rainy afternoon in April, she cut it off.

"There," she thought to herself, "that should change things. Now people will like me for me. Not that stupid curl."

Robert came home that evening and held in tears of sadness as he told Vanessa how beautiful she looked. Then he went on and on about how he actually preferred her hair better that way. But on the inside, Robert was heartbroken. He was confused about why she had done it, but he kept his questions to himself like he thought a good husband should. All of the questions except for one, "So, is this a permanent thing?" Robert asked in a worrisome tone.

Robert slept on the sofa that night, but that was okay. He kind of liked sleeping on the sofa. Those troubled nights were the only chance he got to catch up on the television programs that Vanessa hated.

The next day, Robert left for work, but his words lingered in Vanessa's mind.

"Is this a permanent thing?" She repeated to herself.

Vanessa sat in front of a large vanity mirror in their bedroom, asking herself that same question over and over again... "Is this a permanent thing?" She murmured aloud to no one.

Not the haircut necessarily, but the feeling of being inadequate.

Vanessa was a good mother and, when she was younger, a strong and valuable worker. She put herself through Squirrel School with just the tips she made from working in a small forest diner. It wasn't the best job, but it was work. Hard work some nights. That's actually where she met her sweet and sometimes misspoken husband, Robert.

He would come in for coffee in the morning before his shift would start. He was young, and it was his first job as well. He was driving for a well-known taxi service in town, "The Tortoise and the Fare".

He ordered the same thing every time: hazelnut coffee, four sugars. Robert called it the "Working Squirrel's Speedball". Vanessa called it a "Wrecking Ball" one time, and it made him laugh. He liked her right away; she was funny. Plus, she had that tiny curl in the front of her hair.

Before their babies were born, they would go on weekend trips to exotic places where the food was prepared, but their passion wasn't. Vanessa was quite a spitfire when she was in her youth, and Robert filled his cheeks with it. They were spontaneous, wild even.

Once, on holiday, a park ranger found the lustful young couple getting frisky inside an overgrown oak fern near the entrance sign to a hiking trail. They escaped, but the park ranger's net scratched across Robert's leg as they fled. During conversations at parties, they would tell other couples that the scar on Robert's leg was from a boating trip. They would giggle to themselves and briefly reminisce about that afternoon of ecstasy.

But those days of passion were over, and their spontaneity had dwindled after raising their babies. Now, they'd be lucky if either one of them received a peck on the cheek before bed. Every day felt like the same day as if she was stuck inside the movie Groundhog Day, and Vanessa was no groundhog.

Vanessa went to see the Owl one morning, and they talked about her new habits. The old wise Owl gave her a handful of pills to take each day with breakfast. He assured her that a pill a day would keep those negative thoughts away.

Vanessa didn't believe him. Plus, she kind of likes her negative thoughts. She couldn't explain it.

It almost felt like Stockholm Syndrome.

Depression is a tricky little virus. It's subtle yet overwhelming. It is invisible to your eyes but so loud inside your mind. It's somehow able to set off all of your alarm bells and still rob you.

Vanessa felt so numb that she ached to feel anything at all, which made the bad stuff feel good.

A week later, Vanessa found herself lying in the bathtub. She had decided to take a midday soak. She read in one of her self-help books that this sort of thing would help.

But this particular afternoon, it just wasn't working.

No, instead, she laid in the hot bath, wondering what would happen if she just held her head under the water long enough to escape this never-ending math equation we all refer to as "Life".

What would Robert do if he came home to find his sweet bride floating in the tub? The same bathtub where she gave birth to their two beautiful babies and the three ugly ones they ate. The same bathtub they made love in after their wedding. The same bathtub where they washed their clothes by hand when they first moved into that large redwood tree because they were too poor to own a washer and dryer.

Vanessa had thoughts like these before. Once when she was sweeping, she peered out their front door and wondered what it would be like to feel the wind press against her fur one last time as she fell to the hardened earth's surface. She stopped herself that afternoon because she was a mother to a newborn baby, but not now.

This afternoon, nothing was stopping her. Nothing but the thought of Robert coming home to a bathtub full of cold water and an even colder body floating in it.

When did she become so morbid? Maybe this is who she was her entire life. Maybe she was born this way, or perhaps this darkness crept up inside her over time. Vanessa didn't have those answers.

She laid in the lukewarm water a few more moments before dunking her head underneath.

"My babies will understand," she thought as she began to hold her breath. They might not get it now, but when they get older and realize just how hard life is, surely they will understand it then.

Nobody lives forever, right?

Plus, this way, Vanessa got to choose when to die. Not everybody gets that choice. Hardly anyone does. In those brief underwater moments, she thought of herself not as suicidal but more as a pioneer of death. She thought of herself as, "The Decider". She wasn't going to let life dictate her story. No, she was going to re-write her ending.

A wave of relief washed over her along with the bathwater, and Vanessa had peace of mind for once in her life. Everything was silent under the water. No one could tell her how fat she was because she was weightless. No one would ask how she felt because she felt nothing. The best part of it all, no one would be able to ask her what happened to her beautiful curl and why she cut it off because she would be dead.

A painless solution to life's biggest question: Why are we here?

Are we here for the amusement of others? Are we here to be servants to the workforce? Are we here to follow some word of a god that none of us have ever seen?

Well, none of that mattered now. Those questions were not for Vanessa to answer. Not anymore. She felt free of that pesky never-ending quest. She had reached her destination, and she was finally happy.

"Wait, this isn't fair," she thought. But fair to who? Or whom? She was an educated squirrel, after all.

She felt selfish, leaving Robert behind, but it didn't make sense for her to stick around because of some male squirrel she met at a diner years ago, or, even worse, because of some partnership she agreed upon when the two of them were much younger and happier?

"Animals get divorced all the time," she thought to herself.

Robert was lucky they weren't spiders. If they were, she would bite her husband's head clean off and move on. Or worse, they could be ducks. They are even more barbaric than the spiders.

But this wasn't divorce. She never even had a conversation with Robert.

As Vanessa was debating her decision, her body naturally started to rise out of the water. She had nothing holding her down after all. Nothing, that is, but the guilt of leaving Robert behind.

She began to panic a little. She had already committed to the idea of dying; she couldn't back out now. But Vanessa couldn't fight gravity any longer, and her head shot up out of the lukewarm water as she instinctively began to gasp for air and life.

She felt like a failure.

A coward.

A fraud.

Vanessa scanned the room for something heavy to hold onto so she could stay underwater longer. She was not ready to give up on giving up quite yet.

She locked eyes on a thick book that was laying on the nightstand in their bedroom. Vanessa quickly jumped out of the bath and jolted across the room, dripping water onto the old floors in the big redwood home.

She snatched the heavy book from the top of the nightstand and started to scurry back to the bathtub when she looked down at the book.

"Oh, the irony," Vanessa thought to herself. The book she grabbed was the Bible. The one book that was supposed to hold all the instructions on how to live a meaningful and well-managed life is the same one Vanessa was going to use to drown herself in her mismanaged emotions and self-hatred. She laughed a little at the thought of someone finding her floating corpse that would be clutching that sacred book.

What would they think? Maybe she had a mid-day read and fell asleep? That was fine with her.

Vanessa didn't care much for whatever happens after leaving this life just as long as she wouldn't have to be there to answer any more questions.

Besides, she wasn't much of a religious person anyway, and anyone who knew her knew that. Her close friends would probably have a good laugh at the situation, much like Vanessa was having now.

The truth of the matter was this: It was the most substantial book in their old redwood home. Well, besides the dictionary, but that was in Robert's upstairs office, and she wasn't about to fetch that now.

Vanessa let out a frustrated huff as she sat the Holy Book back down on the nightstand. Then she reluctantly picked up the dense mahogany framed photo sitting next to it. The frame felt like it weighed as much as she did. Plus, it was a gift from Robert's parents. They had gone on a holiday a few years ago to the Southern Amazon in Brazil, and it was all they talked about for three

Christmases.

Inside the frame was one of Vanessa's favorite photographs. It was taken by a cousin who had died in a terrible lawnmower accident a few years ago. The photo was on their wedding day. It was raining the day they got married, so in the photograph, Vanessa and Robert each had one hand bracing a piece of large maple leaf over their heads as they locked eyes and lips in front of a small gathering of their closest friends and family.

"How perfect," Vanessa thought. The weight of marriage and the pressure of being a perfect wife to the only baby that Robert's parents didn't eat would be the thing that would hold her down until she died.

Vanessa laid back down in the lukewarm water once more. She placed the thick mahogany frame firmly on her chest, crossed her arms over the top, and dipped her head down into the water. As air bubbles started to leak slowly out of the corners of Vanessa's mouth, there was just one question left to ask... "What will Robert do without me?"

If you are suffering from depression, I need you to know that you are not alone. I know it might feel that way sometimes. I know that, because that's how I felt for a long time. There is help out there. I promise.

National Suicide Prevention
1800-273-8255

It gets better. Keep swimming.

ABOUT THE AUTHOR

Michael Malone is an award-winning stand-up comedian, film director and writer that is currently based in Los Angeles, California. His blistering humor focuses on breaking down the idiotic ways we deal with life, death, love and sex.

In 2012, Michael won the Seattle International Comedy Competition. From there he was named 2013's "HOT Comic to Watch." In 2014 he was voted one of the "Top Five Comedy Performers" in the U.S. college market.

In 2015 Michael released his second comedy album via Uproar Records titled, "Thirty-One". This album was featured for several weeks on the

New and Noteworthy section on iTunes and became a top ten best selling album on iTunes as well.

Michael has been featured on the second season of Showtime's drama series, "I'm Dying Up Here". Multiple episodes of Comedy Central's "Bad Ass Bitches of History". "Punchlines" on Fox Television, the Bob and Tom Show, XM Radio, 24/7 Comedy Radio, the Fusion Channel, WGN, Comcast on Demand, HULU's "Comedy Time", The CW, and the first two seasons of "Laughs" on Fox Television.

Michael leaped into the film world when he booked the lead in the comedy/horror cult classic film, "Chopping Block" in 2015. The following year he co-wrote, directed and starred in the film, "Bethlehem". This was Michael's debut as a director and writer and the film brought home 16 awards and nominations in the film festival circuit including Best Feature Film, Best Dark Comedy, Best Ensemble Cast and was even named one of the top 10 indie films of 2016.

Michael also wrote, directed and starred in a

short film in 2017 called "Smashing Pumpkins" that was nominated for "Best Film" and "Best Comedy" as well. Later that year Michael went overseas with the Armed Forces Entertainment Tour and performed for the US military in eleven different countries and started writing a monthly column for "Face the Current" Magazine based on his unique storytelling podcast, "Punched Up".

Michael created and voiced the animated series "The Good Doctor" on the Funny or Die network. He also created the NSFW nature show on the Laugh Factory's YouTube channel, "Mother F*cking Nature".

In 2019 Michael produced and directed his own one-hour comedy special that is now available on Amazon and Amazon Prime called, "Laugh After Death".

Since the release in late November of 2019, the special has reached over 2 million views and was trending on Amazon. It is now available in over 60 countries worldwide.

You can find more information about
Michael on his official website
www.MaloneComedy.com

MaloneComedy

MaloneComedy

/MichaelMaloneComedy

© Copyright 2020 by Michael Malone.
All rights reserved. No part of this book may be reproduced in any form or by any electronic or mechanical means, including information storage and retrieval systems, without permission in writing from the author Michael Malone except by a reviewer who may quote brief passages in a review.